PARTY ENTERTAINING

MORE THAN 190 DELICIOUS
APPETIZERS, SNACKS AND MAIN COURSES

PARTY ENTERTAINING

MORE THAN 190 DELICIOUS APPETIZERS, SNACKS AND MAIN COURSES

CRESCENT BOOKS
New York/Avenel, New Jersey

This 1992 edition published by Crescent Books,
distributed by Outlet Book Company, Inc.,
a Random House Company,
40 Engelhard Avenue, Avenel, New Jersey 07001.

Printed and bound in Italy

ISBN 0-517-06956-3

8 7 6 5 4 3 2 1

CREDITS

Designer: Sara Cooper

Contributing authors: June Budgen, Linda Fraser,
Kerenza Harries, Lesley Mackley, Janice Murfitt, Mary Norwak,
Lorna Rhodes, Sally Taylor, Steven Wheeler

Typeset by: Maron Graphics Ltd., Wembley

Color separation by: Fotographics Ltd., J. Film Process Ltd.,
Kentscan Ltd., Magnum Graphics Ltd., and Scantrans Pte. Ltd.

Photographers: Simon Butcher, Per Ericson, David Gill,
Paul Grater, Alan Newnham, Jon Stewart, Alister Thorpe

CONTENTS

Provençal Fish Chowder

New England Clam Chowder

1/4 cup virgin olive oil
1 small onion, finely chopped
1 medium-size leek, finely sliced
2 garlic cloves, crushed
12 ozs. ripe tomatoes, peeled, diced
Bouquet garni
1 bay leaf
8 ozs. potatoes, diced
6 cups fish stock
1 tablespoon tomato paste
1-1/2 lbs. white fish, skinned, boned
1/2 teaspoon dried leaf basil
2 ozs. small pitted black olives, cut in half
Salt and pepper to taste

2 (10-oz.) cans clams
3 slices bacon, diced
1 medium-size onion, finely chopped
1 lb. potatoes, diced
1-1/4 cups fish stock
1-1/4 cups milk
2/3 cup half and half
Pinch dried leaf thyme
Salt and pepper to taste

Drain clams, reserving liquid. Chop clams
and set aside.

Heat oil in a large saucepan. Saute onion, leek
and garlic 5 minutes or until softened. Add
tomatoes and cook about 10 minutes or until
soft. Add bouquet garni, bay leaf, potatoes,
stock and tomato paste. Cover and simmer 15
minutes or until potatoes are just tender.

Fry bacon in a large saucepan over high heat
until fat runs and bacon in lightly browned.
Add onion and saute until soft. Stir in reserved clam liquid, potatoes, stock and milk.
Bring to a boil and simmer about 20 minutes
or until potatoes are tender.

Cut fish in 1-1/2 inch pieces. Add fish, basil
and olives to soup. Season with salt and pepper. Remove bouquet garni and bay leaf before serving. Makes 4 to 6 servings.

Stir in clams, half and half, and thyme. Season
with salt and pepper. Reheat a few minutes,
but do not allow to boil. Makes 6 servings.

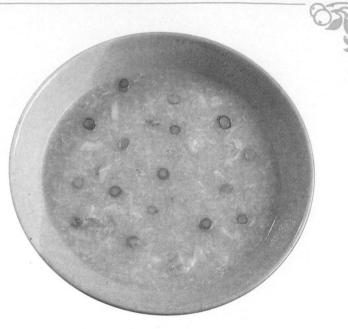

Shrimp Bisque

8 ozs. unpeeled shrimp
1/4 cup butter
1 small onion, finely chopped
2/3 cup dry white wine
3-3/4 cups water
1 fish stock cube
1 bay leaf
Fresh parsley sprigs
3 strips lemon peel
1 tablespoon tomato paste
Salt and pepper to taste
1/4 cup all-purpose flour
Grated nutmeg
2/3 cup half and half

Peel a few shrimp and reserve for garnish.

Process remaining shrimp in a food processor fitted with a metal blade or a blender until finely chopped. Melt 1/2 of butter in a large saucepan. Gently cook onion in butter until soft. Stir in chopped shrimp and cook 4 to 5 minutes. Pour in wine and boil 2 minutes. Add water, stock cube, bay leaf, parsley, lemon peel and tomato paste. Season with salt and pepper and bring to a boil. Simmer, uncovered, 30 minutes, skimming off any froth that forms on surface. Pour mixture through a sieve set over a bowl. Discard bay leaf and parsley. In a food processor fitted with a metal blade or a blender, process solids in sieve and a small amount of liquid to a puree.

Clean sieve and pour puree through sieve into liquid. Clean pan and melt remaining butter. Stir in flour and cook 1 minute. Gradually blend in liquid. Stir in nutmeg and season with salt and pepper. Bring to a boil, stirring constantly. Simmer 3 minutes. Stir in 1/2 of half and half. Swirl remaining half and half on top of soup. Garnish with reserved shrimp. Makes 4 servings.

Crab & Corn Soup

3-3/4 cups chicken stock
1 small piece gingerroot, peeled
2 teaspoons light soy sauce
1 tablespoon dry sherry
1 (15-oz.) can creamed corn
Salt and pepper to taste
2 teaspoons cornstarch
2 tablespoons water
4 ozs. crabmeat
2 eggs, beaten
2 green onions, finely sliced, to garnish

In a large saucepan, combine stock and gingerroot. Simmer 15 minutes. Remove gingerroot and stir in soy sauce, sherry and creamed corn. Season with salt and pepper. Simmer 5 minutes.

In a small bowl, blend cornstarch and water. Stir into stock mixture. Stir in crabmeat and heat until mixture thickens.

Bring mixture to a slow simmer and slowly pour in beaten eggs in a thin stream, stirring constantly. Do not allow soup to boil. Garnish soup with sliced green onions. Makes 4 to 6 servings.

Potage Crème De Fromage

Country Mushroom Soup

2 tablespoons butter
1 medium-size onion, finely chopped
1 stalk celery, finely chopped
1/4 cup all-purpose flour
2 cups hot chicken stock
2/3 cup milk
4 ozs. Camembert cheese, rind removed
1/2 cup cottage cheese, sieved
Salt and pepper to taste

Parsley Croutons:
1 thick slice white bread, crusts removed
Butter
2 tablespoons finely chopped fresh parsley

1 medium-size onion, thinly sliced
1/3 cup brown rice
6 cups chicken stock
3 tablespoons butter
1 lb. fresh mushrooms, wiped clean, trimmed, sliced
1/4 cup plus 1 tablespoon dry sherry
Salt and pepper to taste
Fresh parsley sprigs to garnish

In a large saucepan, combine onion, brown rice and stock. Bring to a boil, then simmer 25 minutes.

Melt butter in a large saucepan. Gently cook onion and celery in butter 5 minutes. Stir in flour and cook 1 minute. Gradually stir in stock and milk. Gradually bring to a simmer and cook 15 minutes. Meanwhile, toast bread on both sides until golden. Cool and spread with butter. Cut in small squares and toss in chopped parsley.

Meanwhile, melt butter in a large saucepan. Gently cook mushrooms about 10 minutes or until golden brown and most of moisture has evaporated.

Cut cheese in small pieces. Add cheese and cottage cheese to soup. Stir 2 to 3 minutes or until cheese is melted. Season with salt and pepper. Garnish soup with parsley croutons. Makes 4 servings.

Add mushrooms to stock. Stir in sherry and season with salt and pepper. Simmer 10 minutes. Garnish with parsley sprigs and serve hot. Makes 6 servings.

Variation: Use 2 or more varieties of mushrooms (button and open or chestnut mushrooms) which have a very good flavor. Wild mushrooms can be used if available.

Ploughman's Soup

2 tablespoons olive oil
1 medium-size onion, finely chopped
1 garlic clove, crushed
2 celery stalks finely sliced
1 carrot, finely diced
1 tablespoon tomato paste
5 cups beef stock
1 (15-oz.) can red kidney beans, drained
3 ozs. small pasta shapes
4 ozs. frozen green peas
Salt and pepper to taste

Heat oil in a large saucepan. Add onion, garlic, celery and carrot. Stir and cook gently 5 minutes.

Add tomato paste, stock and beans. Bring to a boil and simmer 10 minutes.

Add pasta and peas and cook another 7 minutes or until pasta is just cooked. Season with salt and pepper. Makes 4 to 6 servings.

Italian Bean & Pasta Soup

3 tablespoons butter
2 medium-size onions, chopped
1/4 cup whole-wheat flour
2 cups chicken stock
1 cup light ale
Dash Worcestershire sauce
1-1/2 cups crumbled Cheshire cheese (6 oz.)
Salt and pepper to taste
Mild raw onion rings to garnish

Melt butter in a large saucepan. Gently cook onion until soft. Stir in whole-wheat flour and cook 1 minute.

Remove from heat and gradually blend in stock and ale. Return to heat and bring to a boil. Simmer 5 minutes or until thickened. Stir in Worcestershire sauce.

Reserve 1/4 cup cheese. Stir in remaining cheese, a little at a time, over a low heat until cheese is melted. Season with salt and pepper. Garnish with reserved cheese and onion rings. Makes 4 servings.

French Onion Soup

Fresh Tomato & Orange Soup

**2 tablespoons butter
2 tablespoons olive oil
1 lb. onions, thinly sliced
Pinch sugar
5 cups beef stock
1 bay leaf
Salt and pepper to taste
4 thick slices French bread stick
1 teaspoon Dijon-style mustard
3/4 cup shredded Gruyère cheese (3 oz.)**

Heat butter and oil in a large saucepan. Add onions and sugar.

Cook over medium heat about 20 minutes, stirring occasionally, until onions are a deep golden brown. Add stock and bay leaf and slowly bring to a boil. Simmer 25 minutes. Remove bay leaf and season with salt and pepper.

Toast bread on each side and spread with mustard. Ladle soup into 4 heat-proof bowls and top with toast. Pile cheese onto toast and broil until cheese is melted and bubbling. Serve at once. Makes 4 servings.

**1 medium-size orange
1 tablespoon sunflower oil
1 small onion, chopped
1 garlic clove, crushed
1-1/2 lbs. ripe tomatoes, coarsely chopped
2 cups chicken stock
1 teaspoon sugar
1 teaspoon chopped fresh basil leaves
Salt and pepper to taste
1/4 cup whipping cream, whipped, to garnish**

Using a potato peeler, cut 4 strips of peel from orange and reserve for garnish. Grate remaining peel and squeeze juice from orange.

Heat oil in a large saucepan. Cook onion and garlic in oil over low heat 5 minutes. Add grated orange peel and tomatoes and cook over medium heat 5 minutes or until tomatoes are soft. Stir in stock and add sugar and basil. Cover and simmer 15 minutes.

Meanwhile, cut reserved orange peel in thin strips. Drop in a pan of simmering water 3 minutes. Drain and spread on a paper towel. In a food processor or a blender, process soup mixture to a puree. Press puree through a sieve set over a bowl. Clean pan and return puree to clean pan. Season with salt and pepper. Stir in orange juice and reheat gently. Garnish soup with whipped cream and orange peel strips. Makes 4 servings.

Rich Country Chicken Soup

3 tablespoons butter
4 ozs. button mushrooms, chopped
1/3 cup all-purpose flour
2-1/2 cups strong chicken stock
2-1/2 cups milk
12 ozs. cooked chicken, diced
2 egg yolks
2/3 cup half and half
Salt and pepper to taste

Watercress Dumplings:
1 cup self-rising flour
1/2 teaspoon salt
Pinch mixed dried leaf herbs
2 ozs. shredded suet
1 bunch watercress, trimmed, finely chopped
1 small egg, beaten
1 tablespoon water
Chicken stock for cooking dumplings

Melt butter in a large saucepan. Gently cook mushrooms 4 to 5 minutes. Stir in flour, then gradually add stock and milk. Bring to a boil, stirring constantly. Cover and simmer 15 minutes. Meanwhile, to prepare dumplings, sift flour into a medium-size bowl. Mix in salt, herbs, suet and watercress. Add egg and water and mix to a dough. Roll dough in 24 balls. In a large saucepan, bring stock to a boil. Drop dumplings into stock, cover and simmer 10 minutes.

Remove soup from heat and stir in chicken. In a small bowl, beat egg yolks and half and half. Ladle in a small amount of soup into half and half mixture and mix quickly. Pour back into soup and heat gently without boiling until thick. Season with salt and pepper. Using a slotted spoon, remove dumplings from stock and add to soup to serve. Makes 6 servings.

Chicken Noodle Soup

1 chicken carcass, raw or cooked, with giblets
   but not liver
1 small onion, sliced
1 large carrot, sliced
1 stalk celery, chopped
2 to 3 fresh parsley sprigs
1 teaspoon salt
6 black peppercorns
2 ozs. fine vermicelli
1 tablespoon finely chopped fresh parsley

To prepare stock, in a large deep saucepan, cover carcass with cold water and bring to a boil.

Skim off any scum that rises to surface. Add onion, carrot, celery and parsley sprigs and simmer gently 2-1/2 to 3 hours. Strain and cool carcass and stock. Refrigerate overnight. Remove any fat from surface of carcass. Measure 3-3/4 cups of stock into a large saucepan and reheat. Add salt and peppercorns.

Crumble vermicelli into a pan of boiling salted water. Simmer 4 to 5 minutes. Drain and rinse. Place drained vermicelli in a soup tureen and cover with hot soup. Sprinkle with parsley. Makes 4 servings.

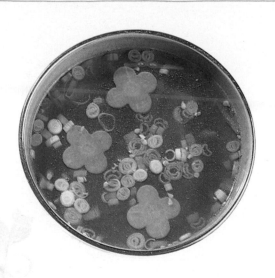

Oriental Chicken Soup

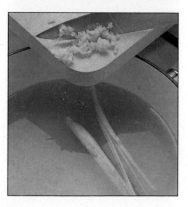

Chicken Consommé:
4 ozs. minced veal
1 carrot, finely chopped
1 stalk celery, finely chopped
1 leek, trimmed, finely sliced
1 thyme sprig
1 bay leaf
7-1/2 cups chicken stock
Salt and pepper to taste
2 egg whites

Soup:
1 garlic clove, finely chopped
1 stalk lemon grass, cut in half lengthwise
Carrot flowers
2 green onions, sliced
2 ozs. cooked chicken breast, shredded
2 ozs. Chinese snow peas, trimmed, cut in strips

To prepare consommé, combine veal, vegetables, herbs and stock in a large saucepan. Season with salt and pepper and begin to heat. Whisk egg whites in a small bowl and pour into stock mixture, whisking continually until a thick froth begins to form. When stock mixture reaches boiling point, stop whisking and lower heat to maintain a very slow simmer. Do not allow mixture to boil. Cook consommé 1 hour.

Line a large sieve or colander with muslin and set over a bowl. Draw scum back from surface of consommé sufficiently to ladle liquid. Ladle clarified stock into muslin-lined sieve. Place a paper towel over surface to absorb any fat. Measure 3-3/4 cups consommé into a large saucepan. Add garlic and lemon grass and simmer 15 minutes. Meanwhile, blanch carrot flowers in boiling salted water 2 minutes. Remove lemon grass and add green onions, chicken and snow peas and simmer 2 minutes. Add carrot flowers just before serving. Makes 4 servings.

Mulligatawny

1 lb. boneless beef stew meat, cut in pieces
7-1/2 cups water
1 (2-inch) piece gingerroot, peeled
2 bay leaves
1 medium-size onion, chopped
1 teaspoon turmeric
1/2 teaspoon chili powder
2 teaspoons coriander seeds, crushed
2 teaspoons cumin seeds, crushed
8 black peppercorns, crushed
1 small cooking apple, peeled, cored, chopped
1 carrot, sliced
2 tablespoons red lentils
2 garlic cloves, chopped
Salt to taste
1 tablespoon lemon juice

Garlic Croutons:
2 thick slices bread
1/4 cup plus 2 tablespoons vegetable oil
3 garlic cloves, crushed

In a large saucepan, cover beef with water. Bring to a boil. Skim surface and add remaining ingredients except lemon juice. Simmer very gently 2-1/2 to 3 hours or until beef is tender. Meanwhile, to prepare croutons, cut off crusts from bread and dice bread. Heat oil in a medium-size skillet. Fry diced bread and garlic, turning bread constantly until crisp and golden. Remove with a slotted spoon and drain on a paper towel.

Remove beef and set aside. Pour stock through a sieve set over a bowl, rubbing vegetables through. Discard pulp. Cool, then refrigerate meat and stock until chilled. Remove solidified fat from surface of soup. Pour into a pan and reheat. Cut beef in small pieces. Add beef and lemon juice to soup and season again with salt, if necessary. Simmer 5 minutes. Garnish soup with croutons. Makes 4 to 6 servings.

Beef & Pasta Soup

6 ozs. capellini (very fine spaghetti)

Beef Stock:
1 lb. boneless beef stew meat, cut in pieces
1 lb. marrow bones or knuckle of veal
7-1/2 cups water
1 medium-size onion, sliced
1 large carrot, sliced
Bouquet garni
1 teaspoon salt
5 peppercorns
1 bay leaf

Parmesan Balls:
1/4 cup freshly grated Parmesan cheese
2 egg yolks

Preheat oven to 425F (220C). In a large roasting pan, bake meat and bones in preheated oven 15 minutes or until brown. Turn meat and bones over and bake another 10 minutes. Transfer meat to a large saucepan. Add water and bring to a boil. Skim off scum which rises to surface. When only white foam is left, add onion, carrot, bouquet garni, salt, peppercorns and bay leaf. Simmer very gently 3 hours. This should yield 5 cups stock.

Strain stock, cool and refrigerate overnight. Next day, remove fat from surface of stock and return to a large saucepan. Reheat stock, seasoning again with salt and pepper, if necessary. When soup simmers, break up pasta and drop into soup. Cook 6 minutes. Meanwhile, to prepare Parmesan balls, mix cheese and egg yolks in a small bowl. Drop 1/2 teaspoonfuls of mixture over surface of soup. Cook about 4 minutes or until balls and pasta are done. Serve at once. Makes 6 servings.

Goulash Soup

2 tablespoons vegetable oil
1 lb. lean beef stew meat, cut in 1/4-inch cubes
1 large onion, thinly sliced
1 garlic clove, crushed
1/2 teaspoon ground cumin
2 teaspoons paprika
1 tablespoon all-purpose flour
5 cups beef stock
1 large potato
1 (14-oz.) can tomatoes, chopped, with juice
Salt and pepper to taste
Sour cream and paprika to garnish

Heat oil in a large saucepan and add beef and onion.

Cook over medium heat 4 minutes or until beef is brown and onion is soft. Stir in garlic, cumin, paprika and flour and cook 1 minute. Gradually add stock. Bring to a boil, then simmer 2 hours.

Dice potatoes. Add potatoes and tomatoes with juice to soup. Season with salt and pepper. Cook 30 minutes or until potatoes are tender. Garnish soup with sour cream and sprinkle with paprika. Makes 6 servings.

Snow Pea Soup

2 tablespoons butter
5 green onions, chopped
12 ozs. Chinese snow peas, trimmed
2-1/2 cups chicken stock
1/2 small head lettuce, shredded
1 teaspoon sugar
Salt and pepper to taste
1 tablespoon chopped fresh mint
2/3 cup crème fraiche
2 slices bread
Oil for frying

Melt butter in a large saucepan. Gently cook green onions in butter 3 to 4 minutes.

Reserve 6 snow peas for garnish and chop remaining. Add chopped snow peas, stock, lettuce and sugar to green onions. Simmer 5 minutes. In a food processor fitted with a metal blade or a blender, process mixture to a puree. Press puree through a sieve set over a bowl. Clean pan and return puree to clean pan. Season with salt and pepper. Stir in mint and crème fraiche and reheat gently. Do not allow to boil. Do not reheat too long or soup will loose its fresh color.

Shred 6 reserved snow peas. Blanch 30 seconds in boiling salted water and drain. To prepare croutons, cut bread in fancy shapes and fry in oil until crisp and golden. Drain on paper towels. Garnish soup with shredded snow peas and croutons. Makes 4 servings.

Pumpkin Soup

1 (3-lb.) pumpkin
2 tablespoons butter
1 medium-size onion, chopped
2-1/2 cups chicken stock
1 teaspoon light-brown sugar
2/3 cup half and half
1/4 teaspoon paprika
Good pinch grated nutmeg
Salt and pepper to taste

Paprika Niblets:
3 slices bread
Oil for frying
Paprika

Discard pumpkin seeds and stringy bits.

Cut out pumpkin flesh and dice. Melt butter in a large saucepan. Cook onion in butter until soft. Add diced pumpkin, stock and brown sugar. Bring to a boil, then simmer 30 minutes. In a food processor fitted with a metal blade or a blender, process mixture to a puree. Clean pan and return puree to clean pan. Stir in half and half, paprika and nutmeg. Season with salt and pepper. Reheat slowly.

Meanwhile, cut out attractive shapes from bread or make rings using 2 cutters, 1 slightly larger than other. Heat 1/4-inch of oil in a medium-size skillet and fry bread until golden. Drain on paper towels, then dust with paprika. Garnish soup with fried bread. Makes 6 servings.

Lobster Bisque

1 (1-1/2 lb.) female lobster
1/3 cup butter
1 small onion, finely chopped
1 carrot, finely chopped
2 stalks celery, finely chopped
2 tablespoons brandy
2/3 cup dry white wine
6 cups fish stock
3 lemon peel strips
3 tablespoons white long-grain rice
Salt and pepper to taste
2 slices toast to garnish

Remove eggs from lobster and reserve.

Remove claws and split tail in half. Remove meat from body, discarding intestinal tube. Crack claws and remove meat. Remove stomach sac and gills from head part. Scoop out green "cream" and reserve. Crush claw shells. In a food processor fitted with metal blade or a blender, process softer body shell and feelers until broken up. Melt 3/4 of butter in a large saucepan. Gently cook vegetables 10 minutes. Stir in broken claw and shells. Pour over brandy and ignite. When flames subside, stir in wine, 3/4 of stock and lemon peel. Bring to a boil, cover and simmer 25 minutes. Cook rice in remaining stock.

Reserve a small amount of lobster meat. In food processor fitted with metal blade or blender, process "cream" and rice. Strain soup into a bowl. Add a small amount of soup to mixture in food processor and process again; whisk into soup. Season and gently reheat. Cut 6 small rounds from toast. Heat remaining butter. Stir in reserved eggs and warm through. Top toast with eggs. Stir remaining eggs and reserved lobster meat into soup. Place toast on soup. Makes 6 servings.

Bouillabaisse

2 lbs. mixed fish (monkfish, cod, squid, mullet)
1 lb. shellfish (shrimp, mussels, scallops)
6 cups water
1 medium-size onion, sliced
1 carrot, sliced
1 stalk celery, chopped
1 bay leaf
Salt and pepper to taste
2 tablespoons olive oil
2 garlic cloves, finely chopped
2 small leeks, trimmed, finely chopped
4 tomatoes, peeled, chopped
Fresh fennel sprigs
3 orange peel strips
Good pinch saffron threads
1 fresh thyme sprig
Salt and pepper to taste

Clean and prepare fish, removing skin and bones. Reserve fish trimmings. Cut fish in chunks. Shellfish can be left unpeeled. Remove heads, if desired. In a large saucepan, combine fish trimmings and bones, water, onion, carrot, celery and bay leaf. Bring to boil. Season with salt and pepper. Remove any scum which rises to surface and simmer 30 minutes. Strain stock into a large bowl, discarding bones and vegetables.

Clean saucepan. Heat oil in clean pan. Cook garlic and leeks over low heat 5 minutes. Add tomatoes and cook 5 minutes. Pour in stock and bring to a boil. Stir in fennel, orange peel, saffron and thyme. When mixture boils, reduce heat and add firmer white fish and simmer 8 minutes. Add shellfish and cook 5 minutes. Season with salt and pepper.

Makes 6 servings.

Smoked Salmon & Dill Soup

2 tablespoons butter
2 shallots, finely chopped
2 tablespoons all-purpose flour
2-1/2 cups milk
1/2 fish stock cube, crumbled
1 cucumber, peeled, chopped
6 ozs. smoked salmon bits
1 tablespoon chopped fresh dill
2/3 cup half and half
Salt and pepper to taste
Lemon pieces and fresh dill sprigs to garnish

Melt butter in a large saucepan. Gently cook shallots in butter until soft. Stir in flour, then gradually add milk. Bring to a boil. Add stock cube and cucumber.

Simmer 10 minutes. Reserve several salmon bits for garnish. Chop remaining salmon bits and add to stock mixture. Cook gently 2 to 3 minutes.

In a food processor fitted with a metal blade or a blender, process soup to a puree. Clean pan and return puree to clean pan. Stir in chopped dill and half and half. Season with salt and pepper and gently reheat. Garnish with reserved salmon bits, lemon pieces and dill sprigs. Makes 4 servings.

Cream of Asparagus Soup

1-1/2 lbs. fresh thin asparagus spears
3 tablespoons butter
1 bunch green onions, trimmed, chopped
2 tablespoons all-purpose flour
3-3/4 cups light chicken stock
2 egg yolks
2/3 cup half and half
Salt and pepper to taste
Additional half and half to garnish

Wash asparagus and cut off tops. Gently simmer tops in salted water 3 to 5 minutes or until just tender. Drain and set aside. Cut off woody ends of stalks. Scrape to remove scales, then chop stalks.

Melt butter in a large saucepan. Cook chopped asparagus and green onions 5 minutes. Stir in flour, then gradually add stock. Simmer about 20 to 25 minutes or until asparagus is tender.

Cool stock mixture slightly. In a food processor fitted with a metal blade or a blender, process stock mixture to a puree. Press puree through a sieve set over a bowl. Clean pan and return puree to clean pan. Beat egg yolks in a small bowl. Whisk a small amount of puree into beaten egg yolks, then return mixture to puree. Stir in 2/3 cup half and half and gently reheat until soup has a creamy texture. Season with salt and pepper. Stir in reserved asparagus tips and heat 2 minutes. Garnish each portion of soup with a swirl of half and half. Makes 6 servings.

Seafood Pâté

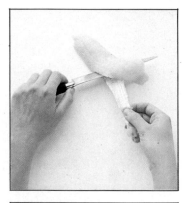

1 lb. white-fish fillets
6 tablespoons butter
6 green onions, chopped
1 garlic clove, crushed
1 lb. uncooked shrimp, shelled, deveined
1/2 lb. scallops, if desired
2 tablespoons cognac or brandy
1/2 cup whipping cream
1 tablespoon lemon juice
1 teaspoon paprika
About 1/8 teaspoon red (cayenne) pepper
Salt to taste

Remove any skin from fish. Pull out any bones, then cut in chunks and set aside.

Melt butter in a large skillet over medium-low heat. Add green onions and cook, stirring, 2 minutes. Stir in garlic, fish, uncooked shrimp and scallops, if desired. Cook, stirring often, until shrimp turn pink and fish flakes. Remove from heat. Warm cognac or brandy in a small saucepan. Ignite, pour over fish mixture and let flames die down.

Stir in cream, lemon juice, paprika and red pepper. Pour cooled seafood mixture into a food processor fitted with a metal blade. Process until smooth. Season with salt. Pour mixture into 1 large or several small serving dishes, cover and refrigerate until firm. Decorate with lemon slices, dill sprigs and cooked small shrimp, if desired. Serve with crackers, melba toast or celery sticks; provide a knife for spreading.

Serves 8 to 10.

Herb & Garlic Mussels

2 lb. mussels in-the-shell
1/2 cup butter, room temperature
2 garlic cloves, crushed
2 tablespoons chopped parsley
1 tablespoon chopped chives
1 tablespoon chopped fresh dill

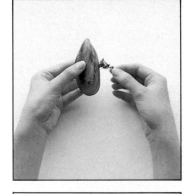

Scrub mussels well with a stiff brush. Pull out and discard beards. Then soak mussels several hours in cold water to cover; discard any mussels with broken shells. Drain well.

In a large saucepan, bring 2 cups water to a boil. Add as many mussels as will fit in a single layer; boil until shells open, then remove from pan. Repeat with remaining mussels, adding uncooked mussels as cooked ones are removed. Lift off and discard top shell of each mussel. Discard any mussels that do not open.

In a bowl, beat butter, garlic, parsley, chives and dill until well blended. Spread mixture evenly over mussels. Cover and refrigerate until ready to cook. To cook, preheat broiler. Arrange mussels in a broiler pan; broil until tops are lightly browned. Serve hot.

Makes about 30, depending on size of mussels.

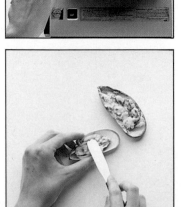

Spanish Shrimp

1 lb. uncooked jumbo shrimp
6 tablespoons olive oil; or 3 tablespoons olive oil
    and 3 tablespoons vegetable oil
1 or 2 small, fresh hot chilies, seeded, cut in
    slivers
3 garlic cloves, crushed

Remove shells from shrimp; remove heads, but leave on tails. Cut each shrimp down center of back, cutting about halfway through so shrimp curls; rinse out and vein. Set aside.

Pour oil into a large skillet; stir in chilies. Place over a medium-high heat. When oil is very hot, add shrimp and garlic. Cook, stirring, until shrimp turn pink. Serve immediately, with crusty bread, lemon wedges and Tartar Sauce.

Makes 4 servings.

Tartar Sauce:
6 tablespoons mayonnaise, preferably homemade
3 green onions, chopped
1 tablespoon drained capers
1 tablespoon chopped sweet pickle
1 tablespoon chopped parsley

In a bowl, stir together mayonnaise, green onions, capers, pickle and parsley. Cover and refrigerate until ready to serve.

Grilled Shrimp

8 uncooked large or jumbo shrimps
1 teaspoon vegetable oil
2 tablespoons soy sauce
2 tablespoons dry sherry
1/2 teaspoon shredded fresh gingerroot
Squeeze of lemon juice
Lemon slices and fresh fennel sprigs

Remove heads from shrimp, but leave on tails. Then cut each shrimp through shell down center of back; be careful not to cut shrimp all the way through. Rinse out sand vein.

Gently spread each shrimp out flat; then thread each one on a metal or bamboo skewer, keeping shrimp lying flat. Set shrimp aside. In a small bowl, stir together oil, soy sauce, sherry, gingerroot and lemon juice.

Arrange skewered shrimp in a large skillet over medium heat. Cook, brushing frequently with soy-sauce mixture and turning several times, until shrimp are pink and well glazed. (Or broil shrimp until done, basting frequently.) Serve whole or cut in pieces; accompany with lemon slices and fresh fennel.

Makes 8.

Taramasalata

2 thick slices crusty bread (about 6 oz. total)
1 (4-oz.) jar tarama
1 garlic clove, crushed
1 tablespoon grated onion
1 egg yolk
2 to 3 tablespoons lemon juice
1/2 cup olive oil
1 ripe olive
Fresh chives
Crusty bread

Trim crusts from 2 thick bread slices. Then place bread in a bowl, pour in enough cold water to cover and let soak for 10 minutes. Squeeze out excess water.

Place soaked, squeezed bread in a food processor fitted with a metal blade. Process to crumb bread evenly. Remove crumbs from work bowl; add tarama, garlic and onion. Process until thoroughly mixed. With motor running, gradually add bread crumbs, processing until mixture is smooth. Add egg yolk and 1 tablespoon lemon juice; process until blended.

With motor running, gradually pour in oil, processing until mixture is very creamy. Season with 1 to 2 tablespoons lemon juice, according to taste. Cover and refrigerate until serving time. To serve, pour in a serving bowl and garnish with olive; accompany with crusty bread for dipping.

Makes 8 to 10 servings.

Salmon Mousse

1 tender cucumber without too many seeds
1 (15½-oz.) can red salmon
1 tablespoon unflavored gelatin
1/2 cup cold water
1/2 teaspoon dry mustard
2 tablespoons distilled white vinegar
1 teaspoon paprika
1/2 pint whipping cream (1 cup)
Melba toast or rye wafers

Trim the cucumber ends. Thinly slice lengthwise. Line a long, narrow 2-cup loaf pan with cucumber slices.

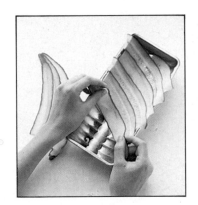

Drain salmon. Discard skin and bones, then place salmon in a food processor fitted with a metal blade. Process until smooth. In a small saucepan, soften gelatin in cold water; then place over low heat and stir until gelatin is dissolved. Pour gelatin over puréed salmon; add mustard, vinegar and paprika. Process until smoothly blended. With motor running, pour in cream, processing only until well mixed.

Pour into cucumber-lined pan, cover and refrigerate until set. To serve, dip pan in hot water up to rim for a couple of seconds. Invert onto a platter and lift off pan. Cut in slices; accompany with melba toast or rye wafers. Place atop melba toast to serve.

Makes 4 to 6 servings.

Prosciutto Roulades

2 oz. ricotta cheese (1/4 cup)
2 oz. Stilton cheese, crumbled
1 tablespoon dairy sour cream
12 very thin slices prosciutto, coppa salami or
   lean cooked ham
1 pear
Lemon juice
Lime slices and dill sprigs, if desired

In a small bowl, thoroughly blend ricotta cheese, Stilton cheese and sour cream. Spread evenly on prosciutto, salami or ham slices, spreading mixture almost to edges.

Peel, quarter and core pear, then cut each quarter lengthwise in 3 thin slices. Brush slices lightly with lemon juice to prevent darkening. Place a pear slice on each cheese-topped prosciutto slice.

Roll up prosciutto slices, cover and refrigerate until ready to serve. Garnish with lime slice and dill sprig, if desired.

Makes 12.

Variation: Substitute an apple or fresh figs for the pear. Peel and slice figs before using.

Chicken Satay

1 lb. skinned, boned chicken breasts
1/2 teaspoon sambal oelek (hot-pepper paste)
1 teaspoon grated fresh gingerroot
2 tablespoons lemon juice
3 tablespoons dark soy sauce
2 tablespoons honey
1 tablespoon peanut butter
1/2 cup water
Cherries and Italian parsley, if desired

Cut chicken in 1-inch chunks and thread chunks equally on 15 bamboo skewers. Set aside.

In a large saucepan or skillet combine sambal oelek, gingerroot, lemon juice, soy sauce, honey, peanut butter and water. Bring to a boil, stirring constantly, then reduce heat and add as many chicken skewers as will fit without crowding. Simmer 10 minutes, basting. Remove from pan and transfer to a rimmed platter. Repeat with remaining chicken skewers.

Simmer sauce remaining in pan until reduced to about 3/4 cup. Pour over chicken. Cover and refrigerate until cold, then serve. If desired garnish with cherries and Italian parsley.

Makes 15.

Fish Pâté

1 quart water
1/4 cup dry vermouth
1 small carrot, chopped
1 small onion, chopped
1 stalk celery, chopped
1 teaspoon black peppercorns
1 teaspoon salt
Sprig of parsley
Small piece of fresh fennel and thyme
1 bay leaf
1/2 lb. fish fillets
2 teaspoons gelatin
2 tablespoons pimiento, chopped
1 green onion, finely chopped
Salt and pepper
Radishes, cucumber, lemon slices, and red and
    black caviar, to garnish

In a saucepan combine first 10 ingredients. Bring to boil; reduce heat and simmer 30 minutes. Add fish; poach 10 minutes until flesh flakes when tested with a fork.

Remove fillets; cool and flake; discarding any bones and set aside. Reduce stock to 1-1/2 cups. Cool. When just warm, sprinkle gelatin on surface, stir to dissolve. Place fish, pimiento, green onion, salt and pepper in a food processor, purée to desired texture, gradually adding fish stock.

Pour into a 3-cup mold, refrigerate until set. To unmold, place container briefly into hot water and turn out onto a platter. Refrigerate. Serve garnished. Store in the refrigerator up to 3 days.

Makes about 2 lb.

Potted Salmon

1/2 lb. smoked salmon
1 cup clarified butter
1/2 teaspoon ground white pepper
Pinch of salt
Fresh chives, to decorate

Blend or process salmon, 3/4 cup clarified butter and pepper.

Blend or process to a fine paste. Add salt to taste and refrigerate until firm. Press into small attractive dishes.

Decorate with fresh chives. Melt remaining 1/4 cup clarified butter, let cool slightly, spoon over potted salmon, making sure it covers completely. Store in refrigerator up to 1 week.

Makes about 16.

Grand Marnier Pâté

1-1/2 lb. pork livers, cleaned, fibrous membrane
  removed
1/2 lb. bacon, cut into pieces
1/2 cup butter, melted
1 medium-size onion, chopped
1/4 cup Grand Marnier (or other orange liqueur)
2 teaspoons grated orange peel
2 tablespoons all-purpose flour
2 eggs, beaten
2 teaspoons salt
1 teaspoon white pepper
1/2 teaspoon powdered cloves
1/2 teaspoon powdered allspice
1/2 teaspoon powdered sage
1/4 teaspoon each powdered mace and powdered
  nutmeg
3 tablespoons whipping cream

Preheat oven to 350F (180C). In a food processor or blender, mix livers, bacon, butter and onion until a smooth purée; add liqueur and orange peel. It may be necessary to do this in batches.

In a bowl, mix together flour, eggs, salt, pepper, cloves, allspice, sage, mace, nutmeg, cream and pureed liver.

Pack into an ungreased 9 x 5-in loaf pan, terrine or pâté mold. Put pan into a larger, deep baking dish. Fill larger baking dish with hot water to level of pâté mixture. Bake for 2-1/2 to 3 hours in baking pan. Cool. Remove pâté from larger baking dish and cool in baking pan.

Orange Glaze:
1-1/2 cups clear chicken stock
1-1/2 teaspoons gelatin
2 tablespoons Grand Marnier (or other orange
  liqueur)

Thin slices of orange, small sprigs of rosemary, celery leaves, black olives and strips of red pepper, for decoration

Warm chicken stock, sprinkle gelatin over surface and stir to dissolve slightly and add Grand Marnier. Decorate pâté with orange slices, small sprigs of rosemary, celery leaves, black olives and strips of red pepper.

Gently spoon the gelatin mixture over pâté a little at a time.

Store in the refrigerator; allow to set 24 hours before using. Will keep up to 1 week well-wrapped.

Makes about 3 lb.

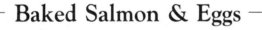

Baked Salmon & Eggs

4 slices smoked salmon
4 large eggs
Salt and pepper to taste
1/4 cup crème fraîche
1 to 2 teaspoons chopped fresh dill
Sprigs of dill to garnish

Preheat oven to 350F (175C). Trim a
small 2-inch-long strip from each piece
of salmon and reserve. Line 4 ramekins
with salmon slices and crack an egg into
each one. Season with salt and pepper.
In a small bowl, mix crème fraîche and
chopped dill and divide equally among
ramekins. Place ramekins in a roasting
pan half filled with hot water. Bake in
preheated oven 15 minutes. Roll reserved salmon strips in small curls and
garnish with salmon rolls and sprigs of
dill.

Makes 4 servings.

Note: Serve with toast.

Prosciutto with Figs

4 ounces prosciutto, sliced very thin
4 fresh figs
4 fig or vine leaves
1 teaspoon honey
1 tablespoon plus 1 teaspoon fresh lime
juice
1 tablespoon plus 2 teaspoons olive oil
1 teaspoon pink peppercorns, slightly
crushed
Shredded lime peel to garnish

Trim any excess fat from prosciutto
and cut in half lengthwise. Cut figs in
quarters. Arrange fig leaves on individual plates and pleat prosciutto on
top. Place figs in prosciutto nest. In a
small bowl, combine honey, lime juice,
olive oil and peppercorns and whisk
well. Spoon over figs and ham and garnish with shredded lime peel.

Makes 4 servings.

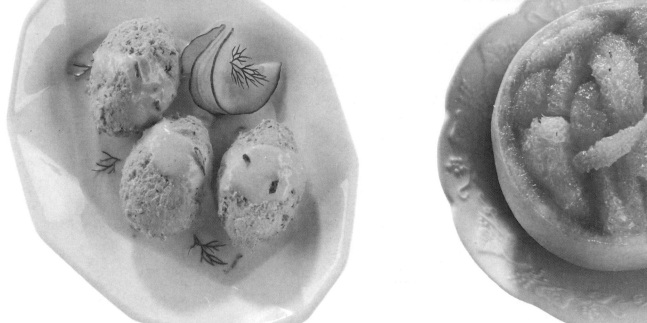

Trout Quenelles

2 large trout, skinned, filleted
1 egg, separated
2 teaspoons chopped fresh dill
1 tablespoon dairy sour cream
Salt and pepper to taste
Pinch ground nutmeg
2 cups fish stock
1 tablespoon lemon juice
1/2 cucumber, grated
1/2 cup whipping cream
1/2 teaspoon cornstarch
Cucumber and lemon twists and sprigs
   of dill to garnish

In a blender or food processor fitted with the metal blade, process trout, egg white, chopped dill, sour cream and salt and pepper 30 seconds. Pour fish stock and lemon juice into a medium-size saucepan and bring to a boil. Reduce heat, until stock is just simmering. Using 2 small spoons, shape trout mixture in 8 ovals and drop into stock. Poach 3 to 4 minutes, until quenelles rise to top of poaching liquid. Remove with a slotted spoon and keep warm. Reduce poaching liquid to 2/3 cup. Add cucumber and boil 5 minutes more until grated cucumber is tender. In blender or food processor, process cucumber mixture until smooth. In a small bowl, mix egg yolk and whipping cream and pour a small amount of cucumber sauce on top. Mix well, then return to pan with remainder of cucumber sauce. Heat gently, stirring constantly, until slightly thickened. Pour sauce on 4 warmed plates and arrange trout quenelles on top. Garnish with twists of lemon and cucumber and sprigs of dill.

Makes 4 servings.

Grilled Citrus Cocktail

2 pink grapefruit
1 white grapefruit
3 oranges
1 lime
1 tablespoon plus 1 teaspoon sweet sherry
2 tablespoons plus 2 teaspoons light-
   brown sugar
1 tablespoon plus 1 teaspoon butter
Sprigs of lemon balm to garnish

Cut grapefruits in half and, using a grapefruit knife, remove pulp and cut in sections. Reserve 4 grapefruit shells. Cut away top and bottom from oranges and lime, then remove all skin and pith. Cut in sections, reserving any juices. In a large bowl, mix grapefruit, orange and lime sections. Arrange fruit in grapefruit shells and sprinkle 1 teaspoon of sherry over each. Sprinkle with brown sugar and top with 1 teaspoon of butter. Broil until brown sugar melts. Top with reserved fruit juices and serve immediately garnished with sprigs of lemon balm.

Makes 4 servings.

Herb Baked Eggs

4 thin slices ham
3 large eggs
1 teaspoon prepared mustard
1/4 cup plain yogurt
3/4 cup shredded Cheddar cheese (3 oz.)
2 teaspoon chopped fresh chives
2 teaspoons chopped fresh parsley
Sprigs of herbs to garnish

Preheat oven to 375F (190C). Grease 4 ramekins. Line greased ramekins with ham slices. In a medium-size bowl, beat eggs, mustard and yogurt. Stir 1/4 cup of cheese into egg mixture. In a small bowl, mix chives and parsley and add 1/2 of mixed herbs to egg mixture. Stir well, then spoon into prepared ramekins. Sprinkle with remaining cheese and herbs. Bake in preheated oven 25 to 30 minutes, until golden and set. Turn out onto serving plates and garnish with sprigs of herbs.

Makes 4 servings.

Note: Serve with hot buttered toast.

Sausage-Stuffed Mushrooms

6 large flat mushrooms
1 tablespoon vegetable oil
12 ounces pork sausage
1 (8-oz.) can ready-cut tomatoes, drained
2 teaspoons tomato paste
2 teaspoons chopped sweet pickle
Salt and pepper to taste
4 ounces thinly sliced mozzarella cheese
Sprigs of basil to garnish

Preheat broiler. Place mushrooms on a baking sheet. Brush tops of mushrooms with oil. Broil mushrooms 1 minute. In a medium-size skillet, fry sausage 3 minutes, stirring to break up sausage. Stir in drained tomatoes, tomato paste and chopped sweet pickle. Bring to a boil and cook until thickened, stirring frequently. Season with salt and pepper. Spoon filling into mushrooms. Top with cheese and broil until cheese is bubbly. Serve at once, garnished with sprigs of basil.

Makes 6 servings.

Strudel Triangles

5 ounces cooked chicken, finely chopped
3/4 cup crumbled feta cheese (3 oz.)
1 small avocado, chopped
2 teaspoons creamed horseradish
Salt and pepper to taste
6 sheets filo pastry, thawed if frozen
5-1/2 tablespoons butter, melted
Sprigs of cilantro to garnish

Preheat oven to 425F (220C). In a medium-size bowl, combine chicken, feta cheese, avocado and horseradish. Season with salt and pepper. Brush 3 sheets of filo pastry with melted butter and lay a second sheet on top of each. Cut each double sheet in 6 (3-inch-wide) strips. Place 1 teaspoon of chicken filling on top corner of each strip and brush pastry with butter. Fold pastry and filling over at right angles to make a triangle and continue folding in this way along strip of pastry to form a triangular bundle. Brush with butter and place on a baking sheet. Repeat with remaining strips. Bake in preheated oven 10 to 15 minutes, until golden-brown. Serve warm, garnished with sprigs of cilantro.

Makes 18 triangles.

Shrimp & Mushroom Barquettes

1 cup all-purpose flour
Pinch salt
1 tablespoon grated Parmesan cheese
8-1/2 tablespoons butter, softened
1 egg yolk
1 tablespoon plus 1 teaspoon water
6 ounces button mushrooms, thinly
    sliced (about 1-1/2 cups)
2/3 cup dairy sour cream
1 to 2 teaspoons dry sherry
3 ounces cooked peeled shrimp, chopped
2 to 3 teaspoons chopped fresh chives
Cooked whole shrimp and triangles of
    lemon to garnish

In a food processor fitted with the metal blade, process flour, salt, Parmesan cheese and 5-1/2 tablespoons of butter 30 seconds. Add egg yolk and water and process until mixture binds together. Wrap in plastic wrap and chill 20 minutes. Preheat oven to 425F (220C). On a lightly floured surface, roll out pastry until very thin. Using a rolling pin, lift pastry and lay over barquette pans. Press down lightly and roll rolling pin over pans to trim off excess dough.

Press pastry down in pans. Prick bottom of each pastry shell and stack on top of each other, three pans high. Top with an empty barquette pan. Bake in preheated oven 15 minutes. Remove from oven and unstack pans. Place pans on baking sheets in a single layer. Return to oven 2 to 3 minutes, until crisp. Cool. In a small saucepan, melt remaining butter and gently sauté mushrooms 1 minute. Stir in sour cream and bring to a boil, stirring constantly until thickened. Add sherry, shrimp and chives and mix well. Cool slightly, then spoon into pastry shells. Garnish with whole shrimp and triangles of lemon.

Makes 12 barquettes.

Note: Barquette pans are small boat-shaped pastry pans.

Kedgeree

12 ounces smoked cod fillets, skinned
8 ounces kipper (herring) fillets, skinned
4-1/2 cups water
1/4 cup wild rice
3/4 cup brown rice
4 tablespoons butter
1 onion, chopped
2 teaspoons curry powder
2 hard-cooked eggs, diced
Juice of 1/2 lemon
2 tablespoons chopped fresh parsley
2/3 cup dairy sour cream
Salt and pepper to taste
Lemon wedges and sprigs of parsley to
    garnish

In a large saucepan, poach fish in 2-1/2 cups of water 10 to 12 minutes, until fish flakes easily. Remove fish with a slotted spoon, reserving cooking liquid, and flake fish. In a medium-size saucepan, combine fish cooking liquid and wild rice. Bring to a boil and simmer 15 minutes. Stir in brown rice and remaining water. Cover and simmer 25 minutes, then drain. In a large skillet, melt butter and sauté onion until slightly softened and transparent. Stir in rice and curry powder and cook 2 to 3 minutes. Stir in flaked fish, eggs, lemon juice, chopped parsley and sour cream and heat through. Season with pepper and salt. Serve garnished with lemon wedges and sprigs of parsley.

Makes 4 servings.

Coulibiac

3 tablespoons butter
1 onion, diced
1 cup button mushrooms, sliced
1/4 cup plus 2 tablespoons cooked white
    long-grain rice
2 tablespoons chopped fresh parsley
Salt and pepper to taste
12 ounces fresh salmon fillet
3/4 cup dry white wine
1/2 cup water
1 egg, hard-cooked
1 (17-1/4-oz.) package frozen puff pastry,
    thawed
1 egg, beaten
1-1/4 cups dairy sour cream, if desired
Lemon twists and sprigs of dill to
    garnish

In a large skillet, melt butter and gently sauté onions until slightly softened and transparent. Add mushrooms and cook 5 minutes more. Remove from heat and stir in rice and parsley. Season with salt and pepper and cool. Place salmon in a shallow saucepan. Pour on wine and water and simmer 10 minutes, until just cooked. Remove salmon with a slotted spoon and flake. Chop hard-cooked egg in small pieces. Roll out 3/4 of pastry in 15" x 10" rectangle and brush with beaten egg. Arrange 1/2 of mushroom mixture down center third of pastry, leaving a 2-1/2-inch strip on top and bottom. Top with 1/2 of flaked salmon, then chopped egg. Cover with remaining salmon and mushroom mixture. Fold sides of pastry up and over top of filling so that the edges overlap; fold ends over top. Brush with beaten egg to seal. Turn over and place coulibiac on a baking sheet with the sealed edges underneath. Preheat oven to 425F (220C). Roll out remaining pastry and cut out fish shapes. Brush pastry all over with egg. Make a small hole in top and decorate with fish shapes. Bake in preheated oven 25 minutes, until pastry is golden. Serve in thick slices with sour cream, if desired, garnished with lemon twists and sprigs of dill.

Makes 6 to 8 servings.

Smoked Fish Lasagne

1 lb. smoked fish fillets, such as haddock
2 cups milk
4 medium-size carrots, cut in small dice
4 celery stalks, cut in small dice
1/3 cup butter
2 cups water
6 lasagne verde noodles
1 tablespoon chopped fresh parsley
Salt and pepper
1/2 cup all-purpose flour
Nutmeg
2 tablespoons Parmesan cheese, grated
Lemon slices, if desired
Fresh parsley, if desired

Put fish and milk into a medium-size saucepan. Bring to a boil; reduce heat to low and cook until fish flakes. Combine carrots and celery in a medium-size saucepan with 3 tablespoons of butter and water. Bring to a boil; simmer until vegetables are tender. Meanwhile, in a large saucepan of boiling salted water, cook noodles until just tender to the bite. Drain; spread out on paper towels. Drain fish, reserving cooking liquid. Flake fish into a bowl. Drain vegetables, reserving cooking liquid. Add vegetables to fish with chopped parsley. Season with salt and pepper. Preheat oven to 375F (190C). Make a Béchamel Sauce with reserved fish and vegetable cooking liquids, remaining butter and flour. Season with salt, pepper and nutmeg. Put a layer of noodles in bottom of a greased 2-quart oblong baking dish. Cover with a third of fish mixture, then a third of sauce. Repeat layers twice, ending with sauce. Sprinkle with Parmesan cheese. Bake 25 minutes or until hot and bubbly. Garnish with lemon slices and parsley, if desired, and serve.

Makes 4 to 6 servings.

Fish & Pasta Pie

12 oz. smoked haddock
12 oz. fresh haddock
1-3/4 cups milk
1-1/4 cups water
2 tablespoons butter
2 tablespoons all-purpose flour
1 teaspoon lemon juice
3 hard-cooked eggs, sliced
Salt and pepper
1 tablespoon chopped fresh parsley
1 cup plain yogurt (8 oz.)
2 eggs, beaten
1-3/4 cups macaroni (6 oz.), cooked
1 cup shredded Cheddar
  Cheese (4 oz.)
Lemon slices, if desired, cut in half
Fresh parsley, if desired

Put smoked and fresh haddock in a medium-size saucepan with milk and water. Poach 5 to 10 minutes until fresh haddock is opaque when tested with a fork. Reserve 1-1/4 cups of cooking liquid. Preheat oven to 375F (190C). Melt butter in a medium-size saucepan. Stir in flour; cook, stirring constantly, 2 minutes. Stir in reserved cooking liquid. Cook until thickened, stirring constantly. Add fish, lemon juice, hard-cooked eggs and chopped parsley. Season with salt and pepper. Pour mixture into a 2-quart casserole. In a medium-size bowl, mix together yogurt and beaten eggs. Stir in macaroni and 1/3 cup of cheese. Pour over fish mixture. Sprinkle with remaining cheese. Bake 25 to 30 minutes or until golden brown. Garnish with lemon slices and parsley, if desired. Makes 4 to 6 servings.

Barbecued Trout in Leaves

4 trout, cleaned, or 8 (2-1/2-oz.) red
    mullet, cleaned
8 grape leaves
1 teaspoon arrowroot
Fresh fennel sprigs and bay leaves to
    garnish

Marinade:
1 tablespoon olive oil
1 tablespoon Seville orange juice
Shredded peel 1 Seville orange
1 garlic clove, crushed
6 cardamon pods, crushed
1/2 teaspoon salt
1/2 teaspoon black pepper
1 teaspoon Dijon-style mustard
2 bay leaves
1 tablespoon chopped fresh fennel

Rinse fish under running water. Pat dry
on paper towels. Score flesh on each
side of fish with a sharp knife. To prepare marinade, in a large bowl, combine all marinade ingredients until well
blended. Immerse fish in marinade,
turning fish to coat evenly. Cover and
refrigerate 1 hour. Remove fish from
marinade and loosely wrap each fish in
a grape leaf. Prepare a barbecue. Arrange fish on a rack in a grill pan. Cook
6 minutes, turning once. Unwrap fish.
Add juices from pan to remaining
marinade and blend with arrowroot.
Pour into a small saucepan and bring to
a boil, stirring constantly. Cook 1 minute. Pour sauce over fish and garnish
with fennel sprigs and bay leaves.
Makes 4 servings.

Buttered Herb Sole Fillets

16 Dover sole fillets
1/2 cup unsalted butter
1 tablespoon plus 1 teaspoon chopped
    fresh tarragon
1 tablespoon plus 1 teaspoon all-purpose
    flour
2 tablespoons half and half
Fresh fennel sprigs to garnish

Marinade:
1 cup white wine
1 tablespoons chopped fresh fennel
1 Red Delicious apple, peeled, grated
2 teaspoons superfine sugar
1/2 teaspoon salt
1/2 teaspoon cayenne pepper

Wash fish. Pat dry on paper towels. To
prepare marinade, in a shallow
flameproof dish, combine all marinade
ingredients until well blended. Add
fish, turning fish in marinade to coat
evenly. Cover and refrigerate 1 to 2
hours. In a small bowl, blend butter and
tarragon. Lay fish flat on a cutting
board. Spread 1/2 of each fish with
herbed butter. Roll up firmly and secure each with a wooden pick. Arrange
rolled fish in a large skillet. Cover and
simmer 5 to 6 minutes or until fish is
tender. Remove fish and keep warm. In
a small bowl, blend flour and half and
half. Strain marinade into flour and
half and half, stirring well. Return to
skillet. Bring to a boil and cook 1 minute. Garnish fish with fennel sprigs and
serve with sauce. Makes 4 to 5 servings.

French Country Cod Steaks

4 (1-inch-thick) cod steaks
1 tablespoon butter, softened
1 tablespoon all-purpose flour
Fresh tarragon sprigs to garnish

Marinade:
1 red bell pepper
1 yellow bell pepper
16 black olives, pitted
4 tomatoes, peeled, seeded, sliced
2 zucchini, sliced
1 red onion, sliced
1 garlic clove, crushed
2 tablespoons olive oil
2/3 cup strong cider
1/2 teaspoon salt
1/2 teaspoon black pepper
1 teaspoon prepared mustard
1 tablespoon plus 1 teaspoon chopped
    fresh tarragon

Preheat broiler. To prepare marinade, place bell peppers on a baking sheet. Broil 10 minutes, turning occasionally, until skins are blistered and charred. Cool bell peppers. Peel and remove stalk and seeds. Cut in strips and place in a shallow baking dish. Stir in olives, tomatoes, zucchini, onion, garlic, olive oil, cider, salt, pepper, mustard and tarragon until well mixed. Immerse fish in marinade, turning fish to coat evenly. Cover and refrigerate 1 hour. Preheat oven to 400F (205C). Bake fish on a baking sheet in preheated oven 25 to 30 minutes or until tender. Remove bones and skin. Pour marinade into a small saucepan. In a small dish, blend butter and flour. Stir into marinade to thicken. Bring to a boil, then cook 2 minutes. Pour sauce over fish and garnish with tarragon sprigs. Makes 4 servings.

Mussels with Basil Sauce

32 fresh mussels
1/4 cup butter, softened
2 tablespoons all-purpose flour
2 tablespoons chopped fresh basil leaves
1/3 cup water
2 tablespoons half and half
Fresh bay leaves and pink peppercorns
    to garnish

Marinade:
3 tablespoons olive oil
1 tablespoon raspberry vinegar
1 tablespoon chopped fresh parsley
2 teaspoons pink peppercorns, crushed
1/2 teaspoon salt
1/2 teaspoon black pepper
1 teaspoon Dijon-style mustard

Scrub mussels thoroughly under running water, scraping shells clean with a small knife if necessary. Pull beards or thin strands from side of shells. In a stainless steel saucepan, heat mussels very gently, covered, until all shells have opened. Remove pan from heat. To prepare marinade, in a small bowl, combine all marinade ingredients until well blended. Stir into mussels and let stand 1 hour. Bring mussels to a boil and cook 1 minute. Discard any mussels that do not open. One at a time, remove empty side of mussel shell and arrange remainder in a shallow serving dish. In a small bowl, blend butter and flour. Stir in chopped basil. Whisk into marinade, add water and bring to a boil. Stir in half and half and pour sauce over mussels. Garnish with bay leaves and peppercorns. Makes 4 to 6 servings.

Salmon in Pastry

4 (4-oz.) salmon steaks, skinned, boned
6 oz. oyster mushrooms
1/3 cup unsalted butter
4 sheets filo pastry
2 teaspoons arrowroot
1 tablespoon half and half
Fresh fennel sprigs, lemon wedges and
    pink peppercorns to garnish

Marinade:
2 teaspoons light-brown sugar
2 tablespoons rosé wine
2 tablespoons raspberry vinegar
2 teaspoons pink peppercorns, crushed
1 tablespoon plus 1 teaspoon chopped
    fresh fennel
1 tablespoon plus 1 teaspoon chopped
    fresh oregano

Arrange fish in a shallow dish. To prepare marinade, in a small bowl, combine all marinade ingredients until evenly mixed. Pour over fish, turning fish to coat evenly. Cover and refrigerate 1 hour. Reserve several mushrooms. Thinly slice remaining mushrooms. Melt 2 tablespoons of butter in a small saucepan. Saute sliced mushrooms in butter. Drain, reserve liquid and let stand until cold. Preheat oven to 400F (205C). Butter a baking sheet. Melt remaining butter. Brush each sheet of filo pastry with melted butter and fold in half. Drain fish well. Place 1 steak in center of each piece of folded pastry. Top each with mushroom slices and wrap up. Place on prepared baking sheet. Brush each parcel with remaining butter. Bake in preheated oven 15 minutes or until pastry is crisp and lightly browned. In a small saucepan, combine remaining marinade, mushroom liquid and arrowroot until blended. Bring to a boil and cook 1 minute. Stir in half and half. Garnish parcels with fennel sprigs, lemon wedges and pink peppercorns and serve with sauce. Makes 4 servings.

Seafood Kebabs

3/4 lb. monk fish (thick end)
3 flounder fillets
3 zucchini
1 small yellow bell pepper, seeded
12 large shrimp, peeled
Fresh bay leaves, lime wedges and fresh
    dill sprigs to garnish

Marinade:
1/4 teaspoon powdered saffron
Finely grated peel 1 lime
1 tablespoon fresh lime juice
1 tablespoon honey
1 teaspoon green peppercorns, crushed
2 tablespoons white vermouth
1/3 cup grapeseed oil
1/2 teaspoon salt
1/2 teaspoon black pepper
6 fresh bay leaves
1 tablespoon chopped fresh dill weed

To prepare marinade, in a large bowl, combine all marinade ingredients until well blended. Cut monk fish in bite-size pieces. Slice flounder fillets in thin strips. Cut zucchini and bell pepper in bite-size pieces. Stir fish, vegetables and shrimp into marinade, turning vegetables and fish carefully in marinade to coat evenly. Cover and refrigerate 1 hour. Soak 6 wooden skewers in cold water. Thread alternate pieces of fish, zucchini and bell pepper onto skewers. Remove bay leaves from marinade and attach a bay leaf at end of each skewer. Prepare a hot barbecue. Cook kebabs over hot heat 5 to 8 minutes, turning only once and brushing with more marinade as required. Garnish with bay leaves, lime wedges and dill sprigs. Makes 6 servings.

Spicy Scallops

12 scallops, cleaned
1/3 cup cider
2 tablespoons all-purpose flour
1 tablespoon butter, softened
2 teaspoons finely grated lemon peel
2 tablespoons fresh lemon juice
1 tablespoon chopped fresh dill weed
Toast triangles, fresh dill sprigs and
    lemon wedges to garnish

Marinade:
1/3 cup dairy sour cream
1/2 teaspoon ground cumin
1/2 teaspoon ground cinnamon
1/2 teaspoon turmeric
1 teaspoon grated gingerroot
2 teaspoons honey
1/2 teaspoon salt
1/2 teaspoon black pepper

In a medium-size saucepan, simmer scallops and cider 1 minute. To prepare marinade, in a medium-size bowl, combine all marinade ingredients until well blended. Using a slotted spoon, remove scallops from liquor. Cut each in half. Add to marinade, turning scallops to coat evenly. Cover and refrigerate 1 hour. Whisk flour and butter into scallop liquor in saucepan. Bring to a boil, whisking until sauce thickens. Stir in scallops, marinade, lemon peel and juice and dill. Simmer until mixture comes to a boil, stirring occasionally. Divide scallops between 6 shells or individual serving dishes. Garnish with toast triangles, dill sprigs and lemon wedges. Makes 6 servings.

Trout in Aspic

4 (8-oz.) trout, cleaned
1/3 cup mayonnaise
2 teaspoon tomato paste
2 tablespoons fresh lemon juice
2 (1/4-oz.) pkgs. gelatin
1 cucumber, very thinly sliced
Salt
Lemon wedges to garnish

Marinade:
1 red onion, sliced
1/2 cup chopped fennel bulb
2 bay leaves
2 tablespoons chopped fresh parsley
2/3 cup white wine
1/2 teaspoon salt
1/2 teaspoon black pepper

Thoroughly rinse trout under cold running water. Dry on paper towels. Arrange trout in a shallow baking dish so they are straight. To prepare marinade, in a medium-size bowl, combine all marinade ingredients until well blended. Pour marinade over trout. Cover and refrigerate 2 to 3 hours. Preheat oven to 375F (190C). Bake trout in preheated oven 15 to 20 minutes or until trout flakes easily. Let stand until cold. Remove trout from marinade. Preparing 1 trout at a time, carefully peel away skin and remove fins, leaving head and tail intact. Carefully remove top fillet of trout. Place bottom fillet on a serving plate. Using scissors, cut through center bone of bottom fillet at head and tail end. Lift off and remove with any remaining small bones. In a small bowl, mix mayonnaise and tomato paste. Spread bottom of fillets with mayonnaise mixture and replace top fillets. Strain marinade into a small bowl. Stir in lemon juice. In a small bowl, blend 3 tablespoons of marinade and gelatin. Set over a saucepan of hot water and stir until gelatin dissolves. Stir into remaining marinade and let stand until just beginning to thicken. Sprinkle cucumber slices with salt. Let stand 15 minutes and drain. Rinse under cold water and dry on paper towels. Brush each trout with marinade. Arrange overlapping cucumber slices to cover each trout from tail to head. Spoon marinade over trout to glaze each trout carefully. Refrigerate until set. Garnish with lemon wedges. Makes 4 servings.

Coconut Spiced Cod

Madras Curried Crab

4 (6- to 8-oz.) cod steaks
Salt and pepper to taste
2 tablespoons vegetable oil
1 onion, chopped
1-1/3 cups shredded coconut
1 (2-inch) piece fresh gingerroot, grated
2 garlic cloves, crushed
2 green chiles, seeded, chopped
1/2 teaspoon chile powder
Grated peel and juice of 1 lemon
2 tablespoons chopped cilantro (fresh
   coriander)
2 tomatoes, peeled, seeded and diced
Oregano sprigs, to garnish

4 cooked medium crab
3 tablespoons vegetable oil
1 onion, finely chopped
3 garlic cloves, finely sliced
1 (1-inch) piece fresh gingerroot, grated
1 large tomato, peeled, chopped
3 green chiles, seeded, chopped
2 tablespoons shredded coconut, toasted
Nut Masala Mixture
1 cup Coconut Milk

Remove large claws from crabs and crack to
make eating easier. Twist off small claws.

Rinse cod steaks; pat dry with paper towels.
Place in a greased baking dish; sprinkle with
salt and pepper. Heat oil in a skillet, add onion and cook, stirring, about 5 minutes, or
until soft. Stir in coconut, gingerroot, garlic,
chiles and chile powder; cook, stirring, 3 to 5
minutes, until golden brown.

Remove the top or back shells, remove finger-
shaped gills and discard. Cut bottom shell in
half with a large sharp knife or cleaver and
use a skewer to remove all the white meat.
Remove and discard the small sack at top of
crab shells and any green-colored matter.
Scrape out creamy brown meat from shells
and add to white meat. Rinse shells thoroughly and set aside.

Stir in lemon peel and juice, cover and simmer 10 minutes to soften coconut. Preheat
oven to 325F (160C). Stir cilantro and tomatoes into coconut mixture and spoon over
steaks. Bake 20 to 25 minutes, until fish just
begins to flake. Serve hot, garnished with
oregano.

Makes 4 servings.

Note: Cover fish with foil during cooking if
coconut begins to brown too much.

Heat oil in a large skillet, add onion and cook,
stirring frequently, about 8 minutes, or until
soft and golden. Add garlic and gingerroot;
cook 1 minute. Stir in tomato, chiles, coconut,
masala, Coconut Milk and reserved crabmeat.
Add crab claws, cover and simmer 6 to 8 minutes, until heated through. Spoon into crab
shells and serve hot.

Makes 4 servings.

Roast Stuffed Turkey

1 (8-lb.) oven-ready turkey with giblets
2-1/2 cups water

Stuffing:
4-1/4 cups soft white bread crumbs
1 large onion, finely chopped
3 celery stalks, finely chopped
Finely grated peel and juice 1 lemon
8 plums, pitted, chopped
2/3 cup red wine
2 cups chestnut puree
1 tablespoon chopped fresh sage
1 tablespoon chopped fresh thyme
1 tablespoon chopped fresh oregano
Salt and pepper to taste
1 lb. bacon
1/2 cup all-purpose flour

Remove giblets from turkey. Place in a saucepan with water. Bring to boil, cover and simmer 1 hour. Strain stock into a bowl; reserve liver. To prepare stuffing, place bread crumbs, onion, celery, lemon peel and juice, plums and wine in a saucepan. Bring to a boil, stirring constantly, and cook 1 minute. In a food processor fitted with a metal blade, process turkey liver, chestnut puree and herbs until smooth. Season with salt and pepper. Add bread crumb mixture and process until evenly blended.

Place 1/3 of stuffing into neck end of turkey. Pull over flap of skin and secure under turkey with skewers or string. Fill cavity of turkey with remaining stuffing. Pull skin over nose and secure with skewers or string. Truss turkey with string, securing wings and legs closely to body, and place in a roasting pan.

Preheat oven to 375F (190C). Cover whole turkey with strips of bacon over breast bone, body, legs and wings to keep moist during cooking.

Bake turkey in oven 2 hours. Remove bacon and cover turkey and pan with thick foil. Return to oven another 1 to 1-1/2 hours or until turkey is tender and only clear juices run when pierced with a knife between legs of turkey. Let stand in pan 20 minutes before removing. Remove any skewers or trussing string and place on a warmed serving dish. Chop crispy bacon finely.

To prepare gravy, blend flour and some stock until smooth. Strain stock into a saucepan and stir in flour mixture. Bring to a boil, stirring until thickened. Cook 2 minutes. Taste and season with salt and pepper and pour into a gravy boat. Serve turkey with bread stuffing and chopped bacon. Makes 10 servings.

Gooseberry Goose

1 (8-lb.) oven-ready goose
2 tablespoons butter
6 shallots, finely chopped
6-1/4 cups soft bread crumbs
2/3 cup gooseberry juice
1-1/4 cups freshly chopped mixed herbs, such
    as marjoram, basil, thyme, rosemary, parsley
1 teaspoon salt
1 teaspoon ground black pepper
12 slices bacon
1 tablespoon Dijon-style mustard
1 cup elderflower wine
1 lb. gooseberries, cooked
1 tablespoon arrowroot
1 tablespoon plus 2 teaspoons superfine sugar
1/4 cup elderberries, if desired

Preheat oven to 425F (220C). Chop goose giblets and reserve liver. Use giblets to prepare stock. Pierce skin of goose. To prepare stuffing, melt butter. Add goose liver and shallots and fry 2 minutes. Reserve 2 tablespoons of bread crumbs. Stir in 1/2 of gooseberry juice, herbs, remaining bread crumbs, salt and pepper until well mixed. Stuff neck end and body cavity of goose. In a roasting pan, cover goose with bacon and bake 45 minutes. Reduce oven to 375F (190C) and bake 1-1/2 hours, pouring off fat during baking.

Chop bacon very finely. Mix bacon and remaining bread crumbs. Brush goose with mustard and sprinkle with bread crumb mixture. Bake another 20 to 30 minutes or until meat is tender. Place on a serving plate. Pour away fat. To prepare sauce, add 1/4 cup of stock to roasting pan and mix with remaining gooseberry juice, wine, gooseberries, arrowroot and sugar. Bring to a boil, stirring constantly and cook 1 minute. In a food processor, process sauce until smooth. Strain and stir in elderberries, if desired. Serve sauce with goose. Makes 8 servings.

Spiced Honey Ham

1 (3-lb.) smoked ham
Finely shredded peel and juice 2 oranges
2 tablespoons honey
1 teaspoon ground mace
1 teaspoon freshly grated ginger
4 oz. kumquats, sliced
2 tablespoons whole cloves
3/4 cup water
1 tablespoon cornstarch

Soak ham in a bowl of cold water overnight. Drain and transfer to a large saucepan. Cover with fresh cold water. Bring to a boil, cover and cook 30 minutes. Drain and cool. Remove skin from ham, leaving a layer of fat on surface of ham. Score fat in a lattice pattern with a sharp knife.

Preheat oven to 375F (190C). Place ham in a roasting pan. In a bowl, mix orange peel and juice, honey, mace and ginger until evenly blended. Brush surface of ham and bake in oven 30 minutes. Remove ham from oven and brush surface with more orange mixture.

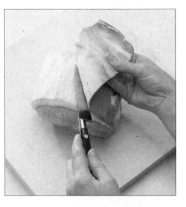

Stud surface of ham with kumquat slices; hold in position with whole cloves. Return to oven another 30 to 40 minutes or until ham is golden brown and tender. Remove and place on a serving dish. Keep warm. To prepare sauce, add water to roasting pan. Stir to mix juices, then strain into a saucepan. Blend cornstarch with remaining orange juice and honey mixture. Add to pan, bring to a boil and cook 1 minute. Serve ham with sauce. Makes 8 servings.

Turkey Vegetable Strudel

9 leaves phyllo or strudel pastry, thawed
1/2 cup plus 3 tablespoons butter
1/4 cup all-purpose flour
1 bay leaf
1 cup milk
2/3 cup half and half
1/2 teaspoon salt
1/2 teaspoon ground black pepper
3/4 cup sliced leek
3/4 cup thinly sliced fennel
1 cup sliced button mushrooms
2/3 cup corn kernels
1 tablespoon plus 1 teaspoon chopped fresh parsley
1 cup diced cooked turkey

Cover phyllo pastry with a damp cloth to prevent drying. To prepare filling, combine 3 tablespoons of butter, flour, bay leaf and milk in a saucepan. Bring to a boil, whisking until thick. Cook gently 2 minutes. Stir in half and half, salt and pepper. Place 2 tablespoons of butter in a large skillet. Fry leek, fennel and mushrooms gently 2 to 3 minutes or until tender. Stir in corn, parsley and turkey. Let stand until cold. Combine thickened milk mixture and turkey mixture.

Preheat oven to 425F (220C). Line a baking sheet with parchment paper. Melt remaining butter. Lay 3 sheets of phyllo pastry flat on a tea towel, brushing in between each sheet with melted butter. Spread with 1/3 of filling to within 1/2 inch of edges; repeat twice more using pastry and filling. Fold in all edges and roll up in a roll with aid of tea towel and roll onto a prepared baking sheet. Brush with remaining butter. Bake in oven 20 to 25 minutes or until golden brown. Cut in slices and serve. Makes 6 servings.

Fruit Pork Pillows

2 tablespoons butter
2 (1-lb.) pork tenderloins, cut in 4 pieces each
3 tablespoons whipping cream, whipped
1 cup chopped dried apricots
1 lb. puff pastry, thawed
2/3 cup sweet cherries, pitted, halved
Fresh sage leaves
Salt and ground black pepper to taste
1 egg, beaten

Preheat oven to 400F (205C). Line a baking sheet with waxed paper. Melt butter in a large skillet. Fry pork pieces quickly 1 minute, turning once, to seal. Drain on paper towels and cool.

In a bowl, whip cream until thick. Fold in apricots. Cut pastry in 8 pieces. Roll out 1 piece very thinly and trim to a square. Spread 1/8 of apricot filling over center. Top with 4 cherry halves, 1 sage leaf and a piece of pork. Season with salt and pepper.

Brush pastry edges with beaten egg; fold pastry over pork and seal well. Invert onto prepared baking sheet and brush with egg. Repeat to make another 7 pillows. Roll out and cut trimmings in holly leaves and berries and decorate each pillow. Brush with egg. Bake in oven 20 to 30 minutes or until pastry has risen and is golden brown. Garnish with remaining cherries and sage leaves and serve hot. Makes 8 servings.

Turkey Risotto

1/4 cup butter
1 large onion, sliced
1 clove garlic, crushed
4 oz. button mushrooms, sliced
1 cup Italian risotto rice
1 teaspoon saffron strands
1 teaspoon salt
1/2 teaspoon ground black pepper
1-3/4 cups turkey stock
2/3 cup white wine
1 small red bell pepper
1 small yellow bell pepper
10 oz. cooked turkey
2 tablespoons shredded Gruyere cheese
1 tablespoon chopped fresh parsley
Small red and yellow bell pepper rings and
     parsley to garnish

Melt butter in a saucepan. Add onion, garlic and mushrooms and cook 2 minutes or until tender. Stir in rice and cook another 2 minutes. Add saffron, salt, pepper, stock and wine. Bring to a boil, stirring constantly, then cover and cook very gently 15 minutes. Broil peppers until skin is charred and peppers are tender. Remove stalk, seeds and skin and cut peppers in fine strips. Cut turkey in bite-sized pieces.

Add turkey and peppers to risotto. Stir carefully to distribute ingredients. Cover and cook another 5 minutes or until rice is tender and mixture is creamy but not dry. Arrange on a warmed serving plate. Sprinkle with cheese and parsley. Garnish with bell pepper rings and parsley and serve hot. Makes 4 to 6 servings.

Red Currant & Clementine Duck

1 (5-lb.) oven-ready duck
Salt
2 tablespoons butter
3 shallots, finely chopped
1-1/4 cups rosé wine
1/2 teaspoon salt
1/2 teaspoon ground black pepper
1 teaspoon whole-grain mustard
1 tablespoon chopped fresh oregano
Finely grated peel and juice 2 clementines
2 tablespoons red currant jelly
3/4 cup red currants, thawed
1 egg, beaten
1-1/2 cups fresh white bread crumbs

Preheat oven to 425F (220C). Remove giblets from duck. Chop liver and reserve. Prepare stock with remainder. Pierce skin all over with a fork; rub salt into skin. Place duck in a roasting pan. Bake in oven 1 hour or until golden brown. Remove and cool 15 minutes. Strain fat from roasting pan. Meanwhile, melt butter in a saucepan. Fry reserved liver and shallots quickly, stirring constantly, until shallots are tender. Stir in wine, salt, pepper and mustard. Bring to a boil and cook 5 minutes. Pour mixture into a roasting pan. Mix with juices and strain back into saucepan. Stir in oregano, clementine peel and juice and red currant jelly.

Using a sharp knife, cut off legs and wings from duck. Slice breast in thin slices and arrange in a warm ovenproof dish. Pour over sauce and red currants. Cover dish with lid or foil. Brush legs and wings with egg; coat each in bread crumbs and arrange in roasting pan. Return to oven 20 to 30 minutes or until crisp and golden brown. Arrange in dish with breast meat and sauce. Makes 4 servings.

Beef-Stuffed Cabbage

2 onions
5 tablespoons vegetable oil
3 garlic cloves, crushed
2 green chiles, seeded, chopped
1 (3-inch) piece fresh gingerroot, grated
1 pound ground beef
1/4 teaspoon ground turmeric
2 teaspoons Garam Masala
1 savoy cabbage
1 (14-oz.) can chopped tomatoes
2 tablespoons lemon juice
Salt and pepper to taste
2/3 cup water
Lemon slices, to garnish

Make sauce, heat remaining oil in a heavy saucepan, add sliced onion and cook, stirring frequently, 5 minutes, or until soft, but not brown. Add shredded cabbage, tomatoes, remaining gingerroot, lemon juice, salt, pepper and water. Bring to a boil and simmer 5 minutes.

Chop 1 onion and slice the other. Heat 2 tablespoons oil in a heavy saucepan, add chopped onion and cook, stirring, over medium heat about 8 minutes, until soft and golden brown. Add garlic, chiles and one-third of the gingerroot; cook 1 minute, then remove with a slotted spoon and set aside. Add beef to pan and cook, stirring, until browned and well broken up. Stir in turmeric and Garam Masala, cook 1 minute, then add onion mixture.

Preheat oven to 375F (190C). Put about 2 tablespoons beef mixture on each cabbage leaf, fold sides in and roll up neatly. Pour a little sauce into bottom of a casserole dish, add cabbage rolls and pour over rest of sauce. Cover and bake 40 to 50 minutes, until cabbage is tender. Serve hot, garnished with lemon slices.

Makes 4 servings.

Cover and cook 20 to 30 minutes, stirring occasionally, until cooking liquid is absorbed; cool. Remove core from cabbage with a sharp knife. Cook whole cabbage in boiling salted water 8 minutes, then drain and rinse in cold water. Leave until cool enough to handle, then carefully peel off 12 to 16 outside leaves, keeping them whole. Finely shred rest of cabbage.

Apple & Elderflower Pork

1 pork loin, boned
1 tablespoons plus 1 teaspoon
    all-purpose flour
2/3 cup water
Elderflowers and apple slices tossed in
    lemon juice to garnish

Marinade:
1-1/4 cups elderflower wine
2 heads elderflowers
1 tablespoon plus 1 teaspoon honey
2 tablespoons almond oil
3 fresh bay leaves

Stuffing:
2 cups chopped cooking apple
2 tablespoons elderflower wine
1 teaspoon honey
1 tablespoon chopped fresh chives
1/2 cup fresh bread crumbs

Trim any excess fat from pork, leaving a thin layer of fat on outside. Score with a knife to make a lattice pattern. To prepare marinade, in a large bowl, combine wine, elderflowers, honey, almond oil and bay leaves. Immerse pork in marinade, cover and refrigerate 4 hours or overnight. Preheat oven to 375F (190C). To prepare stuffing, in a small saucepan, bring apples, wine and honey to a boil. Cook, stirring occasionally, until apple is pulpy and soft and all liquid has been absorbed. Stir in chives and bread crumbs until well blended. Cool. Remove meat from marinade. Pat dry with paper towels. Spread stuffing over center of meat. Roll up and tie securely with thin string in several places. Place in a roasting pan and brush well with marinade. Bake in preheated oven 1 hour, basting with more marinade if necessary. Remove meat from pan. To prepare sauce, stir flour into juices. Add remaining marinade and water. Bring to a boil, stirring constantly. Cook 2 minutes and strain. Cut meat in thin slices. Garnish with elderflowers and apple slices. Serve with sauce. Makes 6 servings.

Variation: If elderflowers are out of season, substitute 2 tablespoons plus 2 teaspoons elderberries or use dried elderflowers.

Beef in Wine

1-1/2 lb. cubed beef stew meat
1 tablespoon butter
6 oz. button mushrooms
2/3 cup beef stock
2 tablespoons all-purpose flour
1 tablespoon tomato paste
Fresh oregano and winter savory sprigs to
    garnish

Marinade:
2/3 cup red wine
1/2 medium-size cucumber, thinly sliced
1 medium-size red onion, thinly sliced
1 tablespoon chopped fresh oregano
1 tablespoon chopped fresh winter savory
1 garlic clove
2 teaspoons light-brown sugar
1/2 teaspoon salt
1/2 teaspoon black pepper

To prepare marinade, in a large casserole dish, combine all marinade ingredients. Stir in meat. Cover and refrigerate 4 hours. Preheat oven to 350F (175C). Strain marinade into a bowl. Melt butter in a large saucepan. Add meat, onion and herbs from marinade and mushrooms. Fry quickly to brown meat. Add marinade and beef stock. Bring to a boil and return mixture to casserole dish. Cover and bake in preheated oven 2 hours or until meat is tender. In a 1-cup measure, blend flour and tomato paste. Stir into beef mixture to thicken gravy. Garnish with oregano and winter savory sprigs and serve hot.

Makes 4 to 6 servings.

Horseradish Steak

1 lb. round steak, cut in thin strips
1 tablespoon butter
2 tablespoons sherry
Fresh thyme sprigs to garnish

Marinade:
1 tablespoon plus 1 teaspoon horseradish
1 tablespoon plus 1 teaspoon plain
   yogurt
2 teaspoons paprika
1 tablespoon chopped fresh thyme
1/2 teaspoon salt
1/2 teaspoon black pepper

To prepare marinade, in a small bowl, combine all marinade ingredients until well blended. Add meat and stir to coat evenly. Cover and refrigerate 1 hour or until ready to cook. Melt butter in a large skillet. Remove meat from marinade and cook quickly 1 minute. Transfer meat to a serving dish. Stir remaining marinade and sherry into pan juices. Bring to a boil, stirring constantly. Pour sauce over meat. Garnish with thyme sprigs. Makes 4 servings.

Juniper Lamb

1 (1-1/4-lb.) loin of lamb, boned, trimmed
1 tablespoon plus 1 teaspoon all-purpose
   flour
1/4 cup water
Lemon wedges, apricots and fresh
   rosemary sprigs to garnish

Marinade:
1 cup rosé wine
1 tablespoon plus 1 teaspoon juniper
   berries, crushed
2 teaspoons angostura bitters
2 bay leaves
1/2 teaspoon salt
1/2 teaspoon black pepper

Stuffing:
1/2 cup fresh bread crumbs
2 ozs. dried apricots, presoaked
2 teaspoons lemon juice
2 teaspoons finely grated lemon peel
2 teaspoons chopped fresh rosemary

To prepare marinade, in a large bowl, combine all marinade ingredients until well blended. Immerse lamb in marinade, turning to coat evenly. Cover and refrigerate 4 hours or overnight. Preheat oven to 375F (190C). To prepare stuffing, in a food processor fitted with a metal blade, process all stuffing ingredients until well blended. Remove lamb from marinade. Pat dry with paper towels. Spread stuffing over center of meat. Roll up and tie securely with cotton string in several places. Place in a roasting pan. Brush well with marinade. Bake in preheated oven 45 to 50 minutes, basting with more marinade if necessary. Remove lamb from pan and keep warm. Add remaining marinade to pan juices. Bring to a boil, stirring constantly. Dissolve flour in water and stir into sauce. Strain sauce into a warmed serving bowl. Remove string from meat and cut in thin slices. Garnish with lemon wedges, apricots and rosemary sprigs and serve with sauce. Makes 4 to 6 servings.

Marinated Ham Steaks

4 (5-oz.) ham steaks
Fresh rosemary sprigs to garnish

Marinade:
2 teaspoons light soy sauce
1 tablespoon sherry vinegar
2 tablespoons peanut oil
1 tablespoon honey
1 tablespoon chopped fresh rosemary
6 whole cloves
1 (1-inch) piece cinnamon stick
1/2 teaspoon black pepper
1 (8-oz.) cooking apple, peeled, grated

Soak ham steaks in cold water for several hours or overnight. Drain and dry on paper towels. Place in a shallow dish. To prepare marinade, in a medium-size bowl, combine all marinade ingredients until well blended. Pour marinade over ham steaks in dish, turning to coat evenly. Cover and refrigerate 1 hour. Preheat a barbecue. Cook ham steaks 3 to 5 minutes, turning once and brushing with extra marinade. Garnish with rosemary sprigs. Makes 4 servings.

Peppercorn Steaks

4 (4-oz.) beef tenderloin steaks
1 tablespoon butter
1 tablespoon whipping cream
Pink and green peppercorns to garnish

Marinade:
1 tablespoon whole-grain mustard
2 teaspoons green peppercorns, crushed
2 teaspoons pink peppercorns, crushed
1 tablespoon tomato paste
1/2 teaspoon salt
2 teaspoons chopped fresh marjoram
2 teaspoons chopped fresh oregano
2 teaspoons chopped fresh basil

To prepare marinade, in a small bowl, combine all marinade ingredients until well mixed. Spread marinade evenly over each steak to coat. Melt butter in large skillet. Cook steaks quickly to seal surfaces. Turn steaks over and cook 3 to 5 minutes or to desired doneness. Remove steaks and keep warm. Stir whipping cream into pan juices and bring to a boil. Spoon sauce over steaks. Garnish with peppercorns. Makes 4 servings.

Peppered Pork

4 (4-oz.) pork sirloin cutlets
Orange slices and fresh ginger mint
   sprigs to garnish

Marinade:
1 small yellow bell pepper
1 small red bell pepper
1 garlic clove
1 tablespoon plus 1 teaspoon olive oil
2 teaspoons grated orange peel
2 tablespoons fresh orange juice
2 teaspoons honey
2 tablespoons chopped fresh ginger mint

Preheat oven to 400F (205C). In a medium-size baking dish, bake bell peppers in preheated oven 10 to 15 minutes or until skin is charred and peels off easily. Cool slightly. Peel bell peppers and remove stalk and seeds. In a food processor fitted with a metal blade, process bell peppers until smooth. Add garlic, olive oil, orange peel and juice, honey and ginger mint. Process to a puree. Place pork in a medium-size baking dish. Pour bell pepper puree over pork, turning pork to coat evenly. Cover and refrigerate 30 minutes. In a large skillet, cook pork 15 minutes or until tender, turning over once. Garnish with orange slices and ginger mint sprigs. Makes 4 servings.

Lime & Pomegranate Lamb

4 (5-oz.) double loin lamb chops
2 tablespoons butter
1 small red onion, thinly sliced
2 tablespoons all-purpose flour
Red currant strands, pomegranate seeds
   and fresh herb sprigs to garnish

Marinade:
2 pomegranates, peeled
Finely grated peel 1 lime
1 tablespoon fresh lime juice
1 tablespoon red currant jelly
1 tablespoon chopped fresh thyme
1/2 teaspoon black pepper
1/4 teaspoon salt

To prepare marinade, scrape pomegranate seeds into a sieve set over a bowl. Reserve a few seeds for garnish. Using a wooden spoon, press pomegranate through sieve to extract all juice. Measure 1 tablespoon plus 1 teaspoon of juice into a small bowl. Reserve remaining pomegrantate juice. Stir in lime peel and juice, jelly, thyme, pepper and salt. Mix well. Place chops in a shallow dish. Brush each chop with marinade to coat evenly. Cover and refrigerate 1 hour. Preheat a barbecue to moderately hot. Cook chops 5 to 8 minutes on each side, brushing with remaining marinade. Keep warm. Melt butter in a small saucepan. Saute onion 1 to 2 minutes or until tender. Stir in flour. Cook 1 minute and remove from heat. Add enough water to reserved pomegranate juice to measure 1 cup. Stir into onion mixture. Bring to a boil, stirring constantly, and cook 2 minutes. Garnish with red currant strands, reserved pomegranate seeds and fresh herb sprigs and serve with sauce. Makes 4 servings.

Pork Tenderloin with Herbs

1 (1-lb.) pork tenderloin, trimmed
1 tablespoon plus 1 teaspoon all-purpose
  flour
Water, if needed
1 teaspoon half and half

Marinade:
2 tablespoons olive oil
1 tablespoon Madeira wine
1/2 teaspoon salt
1/2 teaspoon black pepper
1 teaspoon Dijon-style mustard
1 teaspoon superfine sugar
1 tablespoon grated onion
1 tablespoon chopped fresh sage
1 tablespoon chopped fresh oregano

Place pork in a shallow baking dish. To prepare marinade, in a small bowl, combine all marinade ingredients until well blended. Pour over pork tenderloin, turning to coat well. Cover and refrigerate 2 to 3 hours. Preheat oven to 425F (220C). Bake pork in preheated oven 15 minutes, basting with marinade if necessary. Remove pork and keep warm. Stir flour into marinade in dish. Pour into a saucepan. Bring to a boil and cook 2 minutes, stirring constantly. If sauce is too thick, add a small amount of water. Remove pan from heat and stir in half and half. Slice pork in 1/2-inch thick slices. Serve with sauce. Makes 4 servings.

Rosy Roasted Ham Steak

1 (2-1/2 to 3-lb.) ham steak
Whole cloves
2 teaspoons arrowroot
2/3 cup water
2 tablespoons red currant jelly
Fresh oregano sprigs to garnish

Marinade:
2 cups red currants
2 tablespoons light-brown sugar
3 tablespoon chopped fresh oregano
1 tablespoon olive oil

Soak ham in cold water several hours or overnight. Drain and rinse in fresh water. Place in a large saucepan, cover with cold water and bring to a boil. Cover and simmer 30 minutes. Remove ham from water, cool and remove rind. To prepare marinade, press red currants through a sieve set over a bowl. Stir brown sugar, oregano and olive oil into red currant juice. Add ham and turn in marinade to coat. Cover and refrigerate 1 hour. Preheat oven to 375F (190C). Using a sharp knife, score fat on ham in a lattice pattern. Press cloves evenly into each diamond shape and brush with marinade. In a roasting pan, bake ham in preheated oven 45 to 50 minutes, brushing with extra marinade if required. Cover with foil if surface becomes too brown. Remove ham and keep warm. In a 1-cup glass measure, blend arrowroot and water. Add to pan juices with marinade, stirring to mix well. Strain into a saucepan. Stir in jelly. Bring to a boil, stirring constantly, and cook 1 minute. Pour sauce around ham and garnish with oregano sprigs. Makes 8 servings.

Saffron Lamb Cutlets

8 (2-1/2 oz.) leg sirloin lamb chops
8 sheets fillo pastry
1/4 cup butter, melted
Fresh rosemary sprigs and orange slices
    to garnish

Marinade:
2/3 cup dairy sour cream
2 teaspoons finely grated orange peel
1 tablespoon fresh orange juice
1/2 teaspoon saffron thread or a good
    pinch of powdered saffron
2 teaspoons chopped fresh rosemary
1/4 teaspoon salt
1/4 teaspoon black pepper

Trim excess fat from each chop. Strip off fat and skin from bone above eye of meat, leaving bones completely clean. To prepare marinade, in a small bowl, combine all marinade ingredients until evenly blended. Place chops in a large shallow dish. Spread marinade over both sides of chops. Cover and refrigerate 3 to 4 hours. Preheat oven to 450F (230C). Cover a baking sheet with foil. Arrange chops apart and bake in preheated oven on top shelf 5 to 8 minutes or until marinade is set and chop is tinged with brown. Cool 15 minutes. Brush each piece of fillo pastry with butter and fold in half. Wrap each chop in pastry, leaving bone uncovered. Butter baking sheet. Arrange pastry wrapped chops on buttered baking sheet. Brush with remaining butter and return to oven 10 to 12 minutes or until pastry is crisp and golden brown. Garnish with rosemary sprigs and orange slices. Makes 8 servings.

Spiced Ham Steak

1 (1-1/4-lb.) ham steak
3 oz. creamed coconut
2 tablespoons mango chutney
Juice 1 lime
3 tablespoons dairy sour cream
Lime slices and fresh herb sprigs to garnish

Marinade:
2 teaspoons cumin seeds, toasted
1 teaspoon ground allspice
1/2 teaspoon mustard seeds
1/2 teaspoon white peppercorns
1/2 teaspoon black peppercorns
2 teaspoons grated lime peel
2 tablespoons butter, melted

Soak ham in cold water several hours or overnight. Drain and rinse in fresh water. Place in large saucepan. Cover with water and bring to a boil. Cover and simmer 30 minutes. Remove ham from water. Cool, then cut in thin strips. In a pestle and mortar, combine cumin, allspice, mustard seeds and peppercorns. Crush finely and work in lime peel and butter until well blended and smooth. Rub marinade into ham strips and place in a medium-size bowl. Cover and refrigerate 2 to 3 hours. Heat a nonstick skillet. Fry ham strips quickly 2 to 3 minutes. Stir in coconut, chutney and lime juice. Bring to a boil and cook 2 to 3 minutes. Remove from heat and stir in sour cream. Garnish with lime slices and herb sprigs and serve with sauce.

Makes 4 servings.

Spiced Skewered Lamb

2 (1/2-lb.) lamb shoulder neck fillets
Fresh mint leaves, apple wedges tossed
   in lemon juice and lemon wedges to
   garnish

Marinade:
1 teaspoon ground allspice
1 teaspoon grated gingerroot
1 tablespoon honey
2 tablespoons sherry vinegar
1/3 cup apple juice
1 tablespoon plus 1 teaspoon olive oil
2 tablespoons chopped fresh mint

Trim excess fat from lamb. Cut in very thin strips about 3 inches long. To prepare marinade, in a medium-size bowl, combine all marinade ingredients until evenly blended. Turn lamb strips in marinade to coat each piece evenly. Cover and refrigerate 2 to 3 hours. Meanwhile, soak 8 wooden skewers in cold water. Prepare a barbecue. Thread several pieces of lamb onto each skewer. Cook lamb 2 to 3 minutes, turning once and brushing with more marinade if necessary. Pour remaining marinade into a small saucepan. Bring to a boil. Garnish lamb with mint leaves and apple and lemon wedges and serve with marinade. Makes 4 servings.

Sweet & Sour Spare Ribs

1-1/2 lb. pork spare ribs
Green onion flowers to garnish

Marinade:
1 tablespoon soy sauce
2 teaspoons honey
1 tablespoon dry sherry
3 tablespoons tomato paste
1 garlic clove, crushed
1 small green chili pepper, seeded, chopped
2 teaspoons grated gingerroot
1 (1-inch) piece cinnamon stick
6 cloves
1/2 teaspoon mustard seeds
1/2 teaspoon salt
1 teaspoon black peppercorns

Trim ribs and place in a shallow dish. To prepare marinade, in a small bowl, combine soy sauce, honey, sherry, tomato paste, garlic, chili pepper and gingerroot. In a pestle and mortar, crush cinnamon, cloves, mustard seeds, salt and peppercorns until ground and well blended. Stir spices into marinade until evenly blended. Pour marinade over ribs, turning ribs to coat evenly. Cover and refrigerate 2 to 3 hours. Prepare a barbecue. Cook ribs 5 to 8 minutes, turning once and brushing with more marinade if necessary, until crisp. Garnish with green onion flowers.

Makes 4 servings.

Chicken Bites

1-1/2 lb boneless chicken breasts, cut in
   thin strips
24 kumquats
Cooked pasta, if desired
Sliced kumquats and fresh herb sprigs to
   garnish

Marinade:
2/3 cup plain yogurt, strained
2 teaspoons tomato paste
2 teaspoons Worcestershire sauce
2 tablespoons mango chutney
1/2 teaspoon salt
1/2 teaspoon black pepper
1 tablespoon plus 1 teaspoon chopped
   fresh oregano
1 tablespoon plus 1 teaspoon chopped
   fresh winter savory

Soak 12 wooden skewers in water. To
prepare marinade, in a medium bowl,
combine all marinade ingredients until
well blended. Stir in chicken until
evenly coated. Refrigerate 3 hours.
Prepare a barbecue. Thread a kumquat
and 2 or 3 chicken strips onto each
skewer. Place remaining kumquats on
end of each skewer. Cook skewers,
turning once, 5 to 8 minutes or until
chicken is done. Brush with marinade
during cooking, if necessary. Serve hot
with cooked pasta, if desired. Garnish
with sliced kumquats and herb sprigs.

Makes 4 servings.

Crispy Grapefruit Chicken

8 chicken thighs
Grapefruit segments and fresh rosemary
   sprigs to garnish

Marinade:
1 tablespoon chopped fresh rosemary
1 tablespoon honey
1/4 cup olive oil
3/4 teaspoon cayenne pepper
2 teaspoons finely grated grapefruit peel
2 tablespoons grapefruit juice

To prepare marinade, in a small bowl,
combine all marinade ingredients until
well blended. Arrange chicken in a
shallow baking dish. Cover chicken
with marinade and turn chicken until
evenly coated. Cover and refrigerate 3
to 4 hours. Preheat oven to 425F (220C)
or prepare a barbecue. Cook chicken 20
to 25 minutes or until golden brown
and skin is crisp, basting with more
marinade if necessary. Garnish with
grapefruit segments and rosemary
sprigs. Makes 4 servings.

Curried Chicken Drumsticks

8 chicken drumsticks
1/4 cup butter, softened
1 garlic clove, crushed
1 tablespoon chopped fresh cilantro
1/3 cup fresh bread crumbs
Fresh flat-leaf parsley sprigs and lime
   wedges to garnish

Marinade:
1 teaspoon mild curry paste
2 teaspoons finely grated lime peel
1 tablespoon fresh lime juice
1 tablespoon plus 1 teaspoon creamed
   coconut
1 teaspoon honey
1/2 teaspoon salt
1/2 teaspoon black pepper

Wipe chicken drumsticks with paper towels to dry. To prepare marinade, in a small bowl, combine all marinade ingredients with a wooden spoon to form a paste. Spread marinade evenly over each drumstick to coat. Cover and refrigerate 3 to 4 hours. Preheat oven to 400F (205C). In a small bowl, blend butter, garlic and cilantro until soft and smooth. Spoon into a baking dish and melt in preheated oven. Coat each drumstick evenly with bread crumbs. Roll in butter mixture. Bake 30 minutes or until golden brown and tender. Garnish with flat-leaf parsley sprigs and lime wedges. Makes 8 servings.

Devilled Turkey Breast

1-1/2 lb. sliced turkey breast
1/3 cup butter, melted
1/4 cup tomato sauce
2 tablespoons Worcestershire sauce
1 tablespoon soy sauce
2 tablespoons mango chutney
Fresh watercress sprigs to garnish

Marinade:
2 teaspoons ground ginger
2 teaspoons white pepper
2 teaspoons dry mustard powder
1 teaspoon salt
1 teaspoon curry powder
1 tablespoon light-brown sugar

To prepare marinade, in a plastic bag, combine all marinade ingredients. Shake until well mixed. Shake 1 turkey slice in bag at a time, shaking well to coat evenly with marinade. Cover and refrigerate 1 hour. Preheat broiler. Brush each turkey slice generously with butter. Broil on a broiler pan, turning frequently, 10 to 12 minutes or until golden brown and tender. Remove from pan and keep warm. Stir tomato sauce, Worcestershire, soy sauce and chutney into pan juices. Cook under broiler until sauce bubbles, then pour over turkey slices. Garnish with watercress sprigs.

Makes 4 servings.

Duck with Cranberries & Orange

1 (2-lb.) duck, cut in quarters
2 teaspoons arrowroot
2 teaspoons fresh orange juice
Orange slices, fresh cranberries and
   fresh sage leaves to garnish

Marinade:
1 cup fresh cranberries
2/3 cup water
2 tablespoons plus 2 teaspoons honey
2 teaspoons finely grated orange peel
2 tablespoons fresh orange juice
2/3 cup rosé wine
1 tablespoon plus 1 teaspoon chopped
   fresh sage leaves
1/2 teaspoon salt
1/2 teaspoon black pepper

Trim excess fat and skin from duck. To prepare marinade, in a small saucepan, bring cranberries, water and honey to a boil. Simmer about 10 minutes or until cranberries are tender. Using a wooden spoon, press cranberries through a sieve set over a bowl. Stir in orange peel and juice, wine, sage, salt and pepper. Add duck to marinade, turning duck to coat evenly. Cover and refrigerate 4 hours or overnight. Preheat oven to 425F (220C). Arrange duck in a large baking dish. Bake in preheated oven 45 minutes. Pour remaining marinade over duck. Cover and return to oven. Reduce temperature to 375F (190C). Bake 40 minutes or until duck is tender. Remove duck and keep warm. Blend arrowroot and orange juice in a small saucepan. Pour off most of fat from marinade into a dish. Stir marinade into orange juice. Bring to a boil, stirring constantly, and simmer 1 minute. Pour sauce over duck and garnish with orange slices, cranberries and sage leaves. Makes 4 servings.

Golden Turkey

4 (4-oz.) boneless turkey steaks
1 garlic clove, minced
1/4 cup butter, softened
1/3 cup potato chips, crushed
Fresh flat-leaf parsley and watercress
   sprigs and lime wedges to garnish

Marinade:
12 cardamon pods
2 teaspoons coriander seeds
1/2 teaspoon mustard seeds
1 garlic clove, crushed
1 tablespoon grated lime peel
1/2 teaspoon salt
1/2 teaspoon black pepper

To prepare marinade, remove seeds from cardamon pods. Crush in a pestle and mortar with coriander and mustard seeds until finely blended. Blend in garlic, lime peel, salt and pepper. Cut a slit in each steak to form a pocket. Spread marinade mixture over steaks, rubbing into flesh. Cover and refrigerate 2 to 3 hours. Preheat oven to 425F (220C). In a small bowl, blend garlic and butter. Spread steak evenly with 1/2 of garlic butter, then fill cavities with remainder. Coat steaks evenly in crushed potato chips and arrange in a medium roasting pan, cavity side up. Bake in preheated oven 15 minutes or until golden brown and crisp. Garnish with parsley and watercress sprigs and lime wedges. Makes 4 servings.

Turkey Stroganoff

3 (1/2-lb) turkey fillets
2 tablespoons butter
1 tablespoon olive oil
6 oz. button mushrooms
1 tablespoon fresh lemon juice
2/3 cup pineapple juice
2/3 cup chicken stock
2/3 cup half and half
1 egg yolk
Flesh from 1/2 pineapple, chopped
1/2 cup flaked toasted almonds and fresh
   parsley sprigs to garnish

Marinade:
2 tablespoons all-purpose flour
1/2 teaspoon ground cloves
1 teaspoon ground nutmeg
1/2 teaspoon salt
1/2 teaspoon black pepper
2 teaspoons grated lemon peel

Cut turkey in very thin slices. To prepare marinade, in a medium bowl, combine all marinade ingredients until well blended. Add turkey, turning turkey to coat evenly. Refrigerate 1 hour. Heat butter and olive oil in a large skillet. Cook turkey and mushrooms quickly, stirring occasionally. Stir in lemon and pineapple juices and chicken stock. Bring to a boil, cover and simmer 5 minutes. In a small bowl, beat half and half and egg yolk. Stir into turkey mixture and remove from heat. Stir 1/2 of chopped pineapple. Garnish with remaining chopped pineapple, almonds and parsley sprigs.

Makes 6 servings.

Pheasant in Madeira with Figs & Cherries

1 oven-ready pheasant
1 tablespoon butter
1 fresh fig, sliced, fresh sweet cherries,
   grapefruit segments and watercress
   sprigs to garnish

Marinade:
1 teaspoon honey
2 teaspoons finely grated grapefruit peel
2 tablespoons chopped fresh purple basil
   leaves
2 tablespoons snipped fresh chives
1 teaspoon dry mustard powder
1/2 teaspoon salt
1/2 teaspoon black pepper
2/3 cup Madeira wine
2 tablespoons olive oil
4 figs, cut in quarters
1 cup fresh sweet cherries, pitted
1 tablespoon plus 1 teaspoon all-purpose
   flour
2 tablespoons half and half

Cut pheasant in 4 pieces. Trim excess skin and remove wing tips. To prepare marinade, in a medium-size bowl, combine honey, grapefruit peel, basil, chives, dry mustard, salt, pepper, wine and olive oil until well blended. Stir in figs and cherries. Immerse pheasant in marinade, turning pheasant to coat evenly. Cover and refrigerate 4 hours. Preheat oven to 350F (175C). Melt butter in a large skillet. Fry pheasant quickly to brown evenly. Add marinade, bring to a boil and pour into a large casserole dish. Bake in preheated oven 1 hour or until pheasant is tender. Remove pheasant and keep warm. Spoon fat from marinade. In a small bowl, blend flour and half and half. Add to marinade mixture. Bring to a boil, stirring constantly. Cook until sauce thickens, then simmer 2 minutes. Pour sauce over pheasant and garnish with fig, cherries, grapefruit segments and watercress sprigs. Makes 4 servings.

Chicken Provencal

1 (3-lb.) broiler-fryer chicken
1 red bell pepper
4 tomatoes, peeled, seeded, sliced
Fresh basil leaves to garnish

Marinade:
10 pitted black olives, cut in half
5 anchovy fillets, chopped
3 tablespoons olive oil
3 tablespoons sweet sherry
1 garlic clove, crushed
1/2 teaspoon black pepper
2 tablespoons chopped fresh basil

Cut chicken in half. To prepare marinade, in a medium-size bowl, mix all marinade ingredients until well mixed. Add chicken, turning chicken in marinade to coat evenly. Cover and refrigerate 4 hours. Preheat oven to 425F (220C). Place bell pepper on a baking sheet. Bake in preheated oven until skin is charred and bell pepper is tender. Cool. Arrange chicken in a large baking dish. Spoon a small amount of marinade over chicken. Bake in preheated oven 30 to 40 minutes or until golden brown, crisp and tender. Keep warm. Peel bell pepper and cut in strips. In a small saucepan, combine remaining marinade, bell pepper and tomatoes. Bring to a boil and simmer 5 minutes, stirring occasionally. Garnish chicken with basil leaves and serve with sauce. Makes 4 servings.

Stuffed Quail in Port

4 oven-ready quail
4 stalks celery, chopped
2 leeks, chopped
Fresh mushroom slices and fresh herb
   sprigs to garnish

Marinade:
1/3 cup ruby port
2 tablespoons olive oil
1 tablespoon chopped fresh thyme
1 tablespoon chopped fresh oregano
1 tablespoon chopped fresh winter
   savory
1 garlic clove, crushed
1/2 teaspoon salt
1/2 teaspoon black pepper

Stuffing:
1/4 cup thinly sliced shallots
6 ozs. button mushrooms
1 tablespoon chopped fresh parsley
1/2 teaspoon salt
1/2 teaspoon black pepper
4 slices bacon, chopped

Cut feet and wing tips off each quail. Split quails lengthwise, cutting through 1 side of backbone from neck to tail. Lay quails flat on a cutting board with breast side up. Press down firmly, breaking backbone, to flatten quails. Make a slit between legs through flap of skin. Insert legs and pull through to secure. Loosen skin at breast end of bird to incorporate stuffing. To prepare marinade, in a large bowl, combine all marinade ingredients until well blended. Immerse quail, turning quail in marinade to coat evenly. Cover and refrigerate 4 hours. To prepare stuffing, in a food processor fitted with a metal blade, process shallots, mushrooms, parsley, salt and pepper until finely chopped. Heat a large skillet. Fry bacon until fat runs. Add mushroom mixture and fry quickly, stirring occasionally, until all liquid has been absorbed. Let stand until cold. Insert stuffing under skin of quail. Brush with marinade. Prepare a hot barbecue. Cook quail over hot heat 10 minutes, turning once and basting with more marinade if necessary. Keep warm. Heat remaining marinade in a small saucepan. Add celery and leeks. Cook 2 to 3 minutes or until vegetables are tender. Arrange around quail. Garnish with mushroom slices and herb sprigs. Makes 4 servings.

Basic Crepes

1 cup (4-oz.) all-purpose or whole-wheat
   flour
Pinch of salt
2 eggs
1-1/4 cups milk
1 tablespoon butter, melted

Vegetable oil
Lemon juice and sugar *or* warmed jam

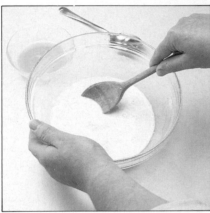

Sift flour and salt into a bowl. Make a
well in the center and add the eggs and
a little of the milk. Beat well with a
wooden spoon, working in all the flour.
Gradually beat in the remaining milk
until bubbles form on top of batter. Stir
in butter.

Add a small amount of oil to a 7-inch
crepe pan – enough to barely cover the
base – and place over high heat. Pour
in 2 to 3 tablespoons batter and quickly
tilt the pan so that the batter covers the
base thinly and evenly. Cook for about
1 minute over high heat until lightly
browned underneath.

Turn crepe with a metal spatula and
cook other side for about 30 seconds.
Keep crepe warm. Continue until batter is used. Serve with lemon juice and
sugar, or with warmed jam.

Makes 8 crepes.

Gruyère & Anchovy Crepes

7-inch crepes

1 (3-oz.) can anchovies, drained
4 oz. Gruyère, Samø or Tybo cheese,
   cut in small, thin strips
2/3 cup sour cream
1 tablespoon lemon juice
Salt and pepper
Chopped fresh parsley and additional
   shredded cheese

Keep crepes warm while preparing filling. Reserve 4 anchovy fillets for
garnish; chop the rest finely. In a small
bowl, combine anchovies, cheese, sour
cream and lemon juice. Season with
salt and pepper.

Divide filling between crepes. Roll up
and place on serving plates. Garnish
with reserved anchovy fillets, parsley
and cheese. Serve at once.

Serves 4.

Salmon Supreme Crepes

7-inch crepes (page 52)

2 tablespoons butter
1 medium-size onion, finely chopped
2 oz. button mushrooms, thinly sliced
2 tablespoons all-purpose flour
2/3 cup half and half
1 (7-oz.) can red salmon, drained and
    flaked
3/4 cup cooked peas
1/2 cup (2-oz.) shredded Gruyere, Samsø
    or Tybo cheese
1 teaspoon lemon juice
Salt and pepper
1/3 cup grated Parmesan cheese
Lemon twists and parsley sprigs.

Keep crepes warm while preparing filling. Melt butter in a medium-size saucepan over low heat. Add onion and mushrooms and cook until soft, about 5 minutes. Stir in flour and cook 1 minute. Remove from heat and stir in half and half. Return to low heat and cook, stirring, until thick and smooth; do not allow sauce to boil. Remove from heat and stir in salmon, peas, cheese, lemon juice, salt and pepper.

Preheat oven to 350F (175C). Divide filling between crepes. Roll up and arrange in a single layer in a shallow heatproof dish. Sprinkle with Parmesan. Bake 25 minutes. Garnish with lemon twists and sprigs of parsley. Serves 4.

Fish Crespolini

7-inch crepes (page 52)

3/4 lb. white fish fillets
2 cups milk
2 tablespoons butter
2 tablespoons all-purpose flour
4 medium-size tomatoes, peeled, seeded
    and chopped
1 tablespoon lemon juice
Salt and pepper
3/4 cup (3 oz.) shredded Cheddar cheese
Watercress sprigs and sliced cherry
    tomatoes

with slotted spoon; reserve poaching liquid. Flake fish and set aside. Melt butter in a small saucepan over low heat. Stir in flour and cook 30 seconds. Remove from heat and stir in reserved liquid and remaining milk. Return to low heat and cook, stirring constantly, until sauce is thick and smooth. Divide sauce in half.

Preheat oven to 375F (190C). Stir fish, tomatoes and lemon juice into half the sauce; season with salt and pepper. Divide between crepes. Roll up and arrange in single layer in shallow heatproof dish. Stir cheese into remaining sauce and spoon over crepes. Bake until sauce is bubbling, about 20 minutes. Garnish with watercress and tomatoes. Serves 4.

Curried Chicken Crepes

7-inch crepes (page 52)

1 medium-size onion, finely chopped
1 tablespoon butter
2 teaspoons curry powder
2 tablespoons all-purpose flour
1-1/4 cups chicken broth
3/4 lb. cooked chicken, diced
1 tablespoon lemon juice
Salt and pepper

Keep crepes warm while preparing filling. Combine onion and butter in a medium-size saucepan. Cook over low heat until onion is soft, about 5 minutes. Stir in curry powder and cook 30 seconds. Stir in flour and cook 30 seconds. Gradually add broth and bring to a boil, stirring constantly.

Stir in chicken and lemon juice. Season with salt and pepper. Cook over low heat, stirring constantly, 10 minutes. Divide mixture between crepes. Roll up and serve immediately. Garnish with slices of green pepper and lemon and sprigs of mint, if desired. Serves 4.

Shrimp & Tuna Crepes

7-inch crepes (page 52)

3 tablespoons butter
1 small green pepper, finely chopped
1 tablespoon all-purpose flour
2/3 cup chicken broth
4 oz. (about 1 cup) peeled and
    deveined cooked shrimp
1 (7-oz) can water-packed tuna, drained,
    flaked
2/3 cup half and half
Salt and pepper
Lemon slices and tarragon sprigs

Keep crepes warm while preparing filling. Melt butter in a medium-size saucepan over low heat. Add green pepper and cook just until softened. Add flour and cook 1 minute, stirring well. Stir in chicken broth and simmer, stirring constantly, until thick. Mix in shrimp and tuna. Stir in half and half and heat through but do not boil. Season with salt and pepper.

Preheat oven to 350F (175C). Divide mixture between crepes. Roll up and arrange in a single layer in shallow heatproof dish. Cover with foil. Bake 15 minutes. Garnish with lemon slices and tarragon sprigs. Serves 4.

Bolognese Crepes

7-inch crepes (page 52)

2 tablespoons butter
1 small garlic clove, crushed
1 large onion, finely chopped
1 lb. ground beef
2 tablespoons all-purpose flour
1 (14-oz.) can tomatoes
2 teaspoons tomato puree
Salt and pepper
1/3 cup grated Parmesan cheese
Sprigs of watercress and tomato halves to
  garnish

Keep crepes warm while preparing filling. Melt butter in a medium-size skillet over low heat. Add garlic and onion and cook until onion is soft, about 5 minutes. Add ground beef and cook, stirring to break up meat, 5 minutes. Stir in flour and cook 1 minute. Stir in undrained tomatoes and puree. Simmer until thickened, about 10 minutes. Season with salt and pepper.

Preheat broiler. Place one crepe on a large heatproof plate. Spread with some of the filling. Top with a second crepe. Repeat until all crepes are used, finishing with a crepe on top. Sprinkle with Parmesan. Broil until lightly browned, about 2 minutes. To serve, cut in wedges. Garnish with watercress and tomatoes. Serves 4.

Sweet & Sour Pork Crepes

7-inch crepes (page 52)

1/2 lb. boneless pork shoulder, cubed
Vegetable oil
8-oz. can pineapple tidbits in syrup
1 tablespoon red currant jelly
1 tablespoon brown sugar
1 tablespoon vinegar
1 tablespoon cornstarch
2/3 cup tomato juice
Salt and pepper
Bean sprouts and green onion flowers, to
  garnish

Keep crepes warm while preparing filling. Heat oil in a medium-size saucepan over low heat. Add pork and cook until tender and cooked through, about 10 minutes. Drain pineapple juice into small saucepan. Add jelly, brown sugar, vinegar and cornstarch and mix well. Add tomato juice and bring to a boil, stirring constantly. Reduce heat and simmer, stirring occasionally, until sauce is thick. Stir in pork and pineapple. Season with salt and pepper.

Preheat oven to 375F (190C). Divide pork mixture between crepes. Roll up and arrange in single layer in shallow heatproof dish. Cover with foil. Bake 20 minutes. Garnish with bean sprouts and green onion flowers. Serve immediately. Serves 4.

Caribbean Crepes

7-inch crepes (page 52)

4 medium-size bananas
2 teaspoons lemon juice
2/3 cup whipping cream
2 tablespoons brown sugar
Grated nutmeg

Keep crepes warm while preparing filling. Peel bananas. Thinly slice one banana; sprinkle with lemon juice and set aside. In a medium-size bowl, whip cream until stiff; set aside about 1/4 for decoration.

Mash remaining bananas in a medium-size bowl. Fold into 3/4 whipped cream along with sugar and 1/2 teaspoon nutmeg. To serve, cut each crepe in half and fold into a cone shape. Fill with whipped cream mixture. Decorate with rosettes of reserved whipped cream and banana slices; sprinkle banana slices with additional nutmeg. Serves 4.

Cherry & Almond Layered Crepes

7-inch crepes (page 52)

1 (14-oz.) can cherries
6 tablespoons cherry jam
1 tablespoon lemon juice
1/2 cup ground almonds
2 eating pears, peeled and thinly sliced
1 tablespoon powdered sugar, sifted

Keep crepes warm while preparing filling. Drain cherries, reserving juice. Measure jam into a medium-size saucepan. Place over low heat and warm just until syrupy. Stir in 2 tablespoons reserved cherry juice, the lemon juice, almonds and pears. Remove from heat and stir in cherries.

Preheat oven to 325F (165C). Place one crepe on a large heatproof plate. Spread with some of the filling. Top with a second crepe. Repeat until all the crepes are used. Bake 10 minutes. Sprinkle with powdered sugar. Cut into wedges and serve immediately. Serves 4.

French Chestnut Crepes

7-inch crepes (page 52)

1 (8-oz.) can sweetened chestnut puree
6 tablespoons orange juice
1 tablespoon lemon juice
1 tablespoon rum
2 tablespoons butter, melted
1 tablespoon powdered sugar

Preheat oven to 300F (150C). Spread each crepe with chestnut puree. Fold into quarters and arrange in shallow heatproof dish. In a small bowl, combine orange juice, lemon juice and rum. Pour over crepes. Cover loosely with foil. Bake 30 minutes. Remove from oven and discard foil.

Preheat broiler. Brush crepes with butter and sprinkle with powdered sugar. Broil until glazed, about 2 minutes. Serve immediately. Serves 4.

Orange Liqueur Gâteau

7-inch crepes (page 52)

1 (8-oz.) can mandarin oranges
2 teaspoons cornstarch
1 tablespoon light honey
1 tablespoon apricot jam
3 tablespoons orange-flavored liqueur
3 kiwifruit, sliced
2/3 cup whipping cream

Keep crepes warm while preparing filling. Drain oranges well, reserving juice; set oranges aside. Mix cornstarch with 1 tablespoon juice. In a small saucepan, combine remaining juice with honey and jam. Bring to boil over low heat. Add cornstarch mixture and stir until thick and clear. Stir in 2 tablespoons liqueur.

Place one crepe on a heatproof plate. Arrange a few mandarin oranges and kiwifruit slices on top and sprinkle with some of honey mixture. Top with a second crepe. Repeat until all the crepes are used, finishing with a crepe on top. Whip cream until soft peaks form; fold in remaining liqueur. Spoon into a piping bag fitted with an open-star tip. Cut gâteau in wedges and pipe rosettes of cream on each wedge. Arrange any remaining mandarin oranges and kiwifruit slices on top. Serve immediately. Serves 4.

Ice Cream Crepes & Chocolate Sauce

Chocolate Sauce:
2/3 cup water
1/2 cup sugar
1/2 cup unsweetened cocoa powder

7-inch crepes (page 52)

1 pint vanilla ice cream
2 tablespoons cherry brandy

For sauce: Combine water and sugar in a small saucepan. Place over low heat and stir until sugar is dissolved. Bring to a boil, then simmer 1 minute. Add cocoa and return to boil, whisking constantly until sauce is smooth. Keep warm.

Cut ice cream into 8 cubes; wrap each one in a crepe. Arrange two crepes on each plate. Sprinkle with cherry brandy. Top with Chocolate Sauce and serve immediately. Serves 4.

Apple-Raisin Crepes with Rum Sauce

Rum Sauce:
1/4 cup unsalted butter
2/3 brown sugar
3 tablespoons whipping cream
1/4 cup dark rum

7-inch crepes (page 52)

1 (8-oz.) pkg. cream cheese, room
  temperature
3/4 cup raisins
1 eating apple, peeled and sliced
Cinnamon

For Sauce: In a small bowl, cream butter and sugar until light and fluffy. Beat in cream and rum. Transfer to a serving bowl.

Keep crepes warm while preparing filling. In a small bowl, beat cream cheese until light and fluffy. Stir in raisins and apple (reserve some of apple for garnish, if desired). Divide mixture between crepes. Roll up lightly and arrange in single layer in serving dish. Decorate with apple and sprinkle with cinnamon. Serve with Rum Sauce. Serves 4.

Basic Omelet

3 eggs
Salt and pepper
1 tablespoon butter

In a small bowl, beat eggs with salt and pepper until just mixed. Set 7-inch omelet pan over low heat to become thoroughly hot.

Add butter to pan. When butter is sizzling but not brown, pour in eggs. Using a fork or spatula, draw mixture from sides to middle of pan, allowing uncooked egg to run underneath. Repeat two or three times so egg rises slightly and becomes fluffy. Cook until golden-brown underneath and top is still slightly runny, about 2 minutes.

Using a metal spatula, fold over 1/3 of mixture away from handle. Holding the handle with the palm of the hand on top, place the pan over a warm serving plate. Shake omelet to edge of pan and tip completely over to make another fold. Garnish with a sprig of watercress and a tomato wedge, if desired. Serve immediately. Serves 1.

Smoked Salmon Omelets

6 eggs
Salt and pepper
2 tablespoons butter
4 oz. smoked salmon, finely chopped
1 teaspoon chopped fresh parsley
1 teaspoon chopped fresh chives
Additional smoked salmon and chives

In a medium-size bowl, beat eggs with salt and pepper until just mixed. Set 7-inch omelet pan or small skillet over low heat to become thoroughly hot. Add a little butter to pan. When butter is sizzling but not brown, add 2 tablespoons of the egg and cook until just set. Lift onto a baking sheet and keep warm. Repeat until all eggs are cooked.

Mix salmon with parsley and chives. Spoon onto one half of each small omelet. Fold over and garnish with additional salmon and chives. Serve immediately. Serves 4.

Seafood Soufflé Omelet

3 eggs, separated
Salt and pepper
2 tablespoons butter
4 oz. peeled and deveined cooked shrimp
1 tablespoon lemon juice
1 teaspoon chili sauce
Lemon slices and fennel or dill sprigs

In a medium-size bowl, beat egg yolks, salt and pepper. In another bowl, beat egg whites until stiff. Fold into yolks. Set 7-inch omelet pan or small skillet over low heat to become thoroughly hot. Add half the butter. When butter is sizzling but not brown, pour in eggs and cook until base is golden-brown, 2 to 3 minutes.

While omelet is cooking, preheat broiler and prepare filling. Heat remaining butter in a small skillet. Add shrimp, lemon juice and chili sauce and heat through. Transfer omelet to broiler until lightly browned, about 30 seconds. Spoon filling over half the omelet. Fold over, cut in half and garnish with lemon and herb sprig. Serve immediately. Serves 2.

Arnold Bennett Omelet

3 eggs
6 oz. smoked cod or haddock fillets, cooked and flaked
Salt and pepper
2 tablespoons butter
5 tablespoons half and half
1/2 cup (2 oz.) shredded Cheddar cheese
Lemon twists and chopped parsley

In a small bowl, beat eggs until just mixed. Stir in fish. Season with salt and pepper. Set 7-inch omelet pan over low heat to become thoroughly hot. Add butter to pan. When butter is sizzling but not brown, pour in eggs. Using a fork or spatula, draw mixture from sides to middle of pan, allowing uncooked egg to run underneath. Repeat two or three times until egg rises slightly and becomes fluffy. Cook until golden-brown underneath and top is still slightly runny, about 2 minutes. Lift onto warm heat-proof plate.

Preheat broiler. Cover omelet with half and half and sprinkle with cheese. Broil several inches from heat source until top is golden and bubbling. Garnish with lemon twists and parsley. Do not fold; serve immediately. Serves 2.

Chicken Liver Omelet

1 tablespoon butter
4 oz. chicken livers, coarsely chopped
1 small onion, finely chopped
1 teaspoon all-purpose flour
2 tablespoons chicken broth
2 teaspoons fresh chopped thyme
Salt and pepper

Basic Omelet (page 59)

Prepare filling before making omelet.
Melt butter in a small skillet over low
heat. Add chicken livers and onion and
stir until onion is soft and golden, about 3
minutes. Stir in flour, broth and thyme.
Bring to boil, then simmer 10 minutes.
Season with salt and pepper.

Make omelet. Spoon filling over half the
omelet. Fold over and serve immediately.
Garnish with sprigs of thyme and grapes,
if desired. Serves 1.

Tortilla Loaf

4 lean slices bacon, chopped
1 tablespoon butter
1/2 lb. potatoes, cooked and diced
6 eggs
Salt and pepper
4 long bread rolls
Butter
Lettuce leaves

In a medium-size skillet over medium-
high heat, combine bacon and butter.
Cook until bacon is soft. Reduce heat to
medium, stir in potatoes and cook until
golden. In a medium-size bowl, beat eggs
with salt and pepper until just mixed.
Pour over potatoes and cook, lifting with
a fork, until eggs are just set.

Split rolls lengthwise; spread cut sides
lightly with butter. Place a lettuce leaf on
bottom half of each roll. Cut egg mixture
into slices and place on lettuce. Cover
with top half of roll. Serve hot or cold.
Serves 4.

Ham & Watercress Omelet

1 tablespoon butter
2 oz. (1/4 cup) cooked ham, finely
  chopped
1/4 cup finely chopped watercress leaves
Salt and pepper

Basic Omelet (page 59)

Prepare filling before making omelet.
Melt butter in a small skillet over low
heat. Add ham and watercress and shake
until warmed through, about 1 minute.
Remove from heat and season well with
salt and pepper.

Make omelet. Spoon ham mixture over
half the omelet. Fold over and serve immediately. Garnish with a sprig of watercress and rolls of thickly-sliced ham, if
desired. Serves 1.

Bacon & Mushroom Omelet

1 tablespoon butter
2 lean slices bacon, diced
3/4 cup thinly sliced mushrooms
3 eggs
Salt and pepper
1 medium-size tomato, peeled and sliced

Melt butter in a 7-inch omelet pan over
low heat. Add bacon and cook 2 minutes.
Stir in mushrooms and cook 2 minutes.

In a small bowl, beat eggs with salt and
pepper until just mixed. Pour into pan
with bacon and mushrooms and top with
tomato slices. As eggs cook, draw the
mixture from edge of pan to center so
uncooked egg runs underneath. When top
is just set, slide omelet flat onto serving
plate. Garnish with a sprig of mint and
mushroom slices, if desired. Serves 1.

Egg Foo Young

4 eggs
1 tablespoon soy sauce
1 tablespoon vegetable oil
2 oz. cooked ham, shredded
3 oz. bean sprouts
4 green onions, finely chopped

Preheat broiler. In a small bowl, beat eggs with soy sauce until just mixed. Set 7-inch omelet pan over low heat to become thoroughly hot. Add oil. When hot, stir in ham, bean sprouts and onion. Cook, stirring constantly, 2 minutes.

Pour in eggs and stir with a fork until mixture has just set. Broil until golden-brown, about 1 minute. Garnish with green onions, if desired. Serves 2.

Spanish Omelet

1 tablespoon olive oil
2 medium-size tomatoes, peeled and
    quartered
1 small onion, finely chopped
1 small green pepper, finely chopped
1 thick slice cooked ham, diced
1 medium-size potato, cooked, diced
1 garlic clove, crushed
4 stuffed green olives, sliced
4 eggs
Salt and pepper

Heat oil in a large skillet over low heat. Add tomatoes, onion, green pepper, ham, potato and garlic. Cook, stirring often, until vegetables are tender, 7 to 8 minutes. Stir in olives.

Preheat broiler. In a small bowl, beat eggs with salt and pepper until just mixed. Pour over vegetables and cook 3 minutes. Broil until top is golden-brown, about 1 minute. Cut omelet in half and slide each half onto a hot serving plate. Serves 2.

Pipérade

1/4 cup butter
1 large onion, finely sliced
2 green peppers, cut into strips
1 garlic clove, crushed
1 lb. tomatoes, peeled and chopped
Salt and pepper
1/4 lb. sliced bacon
6 eggs
Parsley sprig

Melt butter in a large skillet over low heat. Add onion and cook 5 minutes. Add green pepper and garlic and cook 5 minutes. Add tomatoes, salt and pepper. Cover and cook 20 minutes.

Meanwhile, grill or fry bacon; keep hot. In a medium-size bowl, beat eggs thoroughly. Add to tomato mixture and, using a fork, lift eggs constantly until just set. Spoon onto a warm flat serving dish and cover with bacon. Garnish with parsley sprig. Serves 4.

Italian Pizza Omelet

1 tablespoon vegetable oil
1 small onion, finely chopped
1 (7-oz.) can tomatoes
Pinch of marjoram
Salt and pepper

2 Basic Omelets (page 59)

2 oz. button mushrooms, thinly sliced
1 medium-size tomato, sliced
1 oz. Mozzarella cheese, thinly sliced
4 thin slices salami, halved
Marjoram sprigs and capers

Prepare topping before making omelets. Heat oil in a small saucepan over low heat. Add onion and cook 3 minutes. Add undrained tomatoes, marjoram, salt and pepper. Simmer uncovered until reduced by half, about 10 minutes.

Preheat broiler. Make omelets. When 2/3 cooked, spoon half the tomato mixture over each one. Top each with half the mushrooms, tomato and cheese. Broil until cheese is melted and top of egg is set, about 1 minute. Roll salami halves into cones and place 4 on each omelet. Garnish with marjoram and capers. Serve immediately. Serves 2.

Omelet-Meringue Surprise

6 eggs
2 tablespoons sugar
2 almond macaroons, crushed
2 tablespoons half and half
1 tablespoon butter
5 tablespoons blackberry or black currant jam
1/4 cup finely chopped walnuts

Topping:
2 egg whites
1/2 cup sugar
2 tablespoons powdered sugar, sifted

Preheat oven to 425F (220C). In a medium-size bowl, beat eggs, sugar, macaroons and half and half until thick and creamy. Set 7-inch omelet pan over low heat to become thoroughly hot. Add half the butter and heat until sizzling but not brown. Pour in half the egg mixture. Cook until just set. Lift onto a warm heatproof plate. Repeat with remaining butter and egg mixture. Warm jam in a small saucepan over low heat. Stir in walnuts. Spread over first omelet; top with second omelet.

For topping: In a bowl, beat egg whites until stiff; gradually beat in sugar. Pipe meringue over omelets, *sealing completely* (do not leave even a pin-sized area unsealed or meringue will begin to shrink). Sprinkle with powdered sugar. Bake 3 minutes. Serve immediately. Serves 4.

Christmas Omelet

6 eggs, separated
2 tablespoons sugar
Grated zest (colored part only) of 1 orange
4 tablespoons rum
2 tablespoons butter
6 tablespoons fruit mincemeat
2 teaspoons powdered sugar, sifted

In a medium-size bowl, beat egg yolks with sugar, zest and 1 tablespoon of the rum. In a large bowl, beat egg whites until stiff. Fold into yolks. Set an 8-inch omelet pan over low heat to become thoroughly hot. Add butter and heat until sizzling but not brown. Add egg mixture; cook until golden-brown underneath, 4 to 5 minutes.

Preheat broiler. Heat mincemeat in a small saucepan until lukewarm. Spread on half the omelet. Fold over and lift onto a warm heatproof plate. Sprinkle with powdered sugar. Broil until sugar is melted and top is glazed, about 30 seconds. In a small pan, gently warm remaining rum. Pour over omelet and ignite quickly with a match. Serves 3 to 4.

Stuffed Tomato Salad

12 very small firm tomatoes
About 6 tablespoons small-curd cottage
   cheese or ricotta cheese
1 tablespoon half and half
2 oz. smoked or smoked spiced ham,
   finely chopped
1 (1-inch) length cucumber, peeled, finely
   chopped
2 teaspoons chopped fresh dill
Fresh dill sprigs
8 to 12 small lettuce leaves of your choice
1 to 2 tablespoons herb vinaigrette

Using a serrated knife, cut tops off tomatoes. Set tops aside. With knife tip, carefully cut around inside of each tomato; then scoop out center of each tomato with a small spoon. (Discard centers or reserve for another use.) Turn tomato shells upside down on paper towels to drain. In a bowl, beat cottage or ricotta cheese and half and half until smooth. Stir in ham, cucumber and chopped dill. Carefully spoon into tomatoes and replace tops. Garnish each with a dill sprig. Toss lettuce leaves in vinaigrette and arrange on 4 plates. Put 3 tomatoes on each plate and serve. Makes 4 servings.

Variation: If desired, cut tomatoes as shown in the photograph, leaving a "handle" on each one rather than cutting off tops completely. Carefully scoop out centers and pulp beneath "handle." Lay shells on their sides to drain before stuffing them.

Celery Root & Mussels

2 tablespoons lemon juice
1-1/2 lbs. celery root
2 lbs. live mussels, scrubbed, de-
   bearded
1 cup dry white wine
Remoulade Sauce, see below

Remoulade Sauce:
5 tablespoons mayonnaise
2 teaspoons chopped sweet or dill pickles
1 teaspoon chopped capers
1 teaspoon chopped parsley
1 teaspoon anchovy paste

Half-fill a large saucepan with water; add lemon juice. Bring to a boil. Meanwhile, scrub and peel celery root, then cut into thin slices; immediately drop slices into boiling water-lemon juice mixture. Reduce heat, cover and simmer 4 to 5 minutes or just until tender. Drain; cut slices into thin strips, place in a bowl and let cool. Place mussels in a large saucepan, add wine, cover and cook over high heat until mussels open. Remove from heat. Discard any mussels that remain closed. Drain mussels, reserving cooking liquid. Reserve a few mussels in their shells for garnish; remove remainder from shells and add to celery root. To prepare Remoulade Sauce, place all sauce ingredients in a bowl with 2 to 3 tablespoons of the reserved mussel cooking liquid. Mix well to make a sauce with the consistency of whipping cream. Stir sauce into celery root and mussels. Spoon into a serving dish or individual dishes. Garnish with reserved mussels in the shell. Makes 4 servings.

Kipper Salad

3 large undyed kippers
2 tablespoons light olive oil
1/4 cup lemon juice
1 teaspoon sugar
1 onion, sliced, separated into rings
1 bay leaf
About 1 cup alfalfa or other sprouts
1 lemon, thinly sliced

Bone and skin kippers. Slice flesh and place in a glass dish. Pour oil and lemon juice over fish; top with sugar, onion and bay leaf. Mix well. Cover and refrigerate 24 hours, stirring occasionally. Discard bay leaf. Drain kipper mixture and divide among 4 plates. Garnish each serving with sprouts and lemon slices. Makes 4 servings.

Indonesian Seafood Starter

8 oz. small whole squid
12 oz. uncooked shrimp in the shell
1 tablespoon sunflower oil
1 small onion, finely chopped
1 garlic clove, crushed
3 tomatoes, peeled, chopped
1 tablespoon dark soy sauce
1 teaspoon ground ginger
1 small fresh green chili, seeded, finely chopped
1 tablespoon red wine vinegar
1/2 red bell pepper, seeded, cut into thin strips
1/2 green bell pepper, seeded, cut into thin strips

To clean squid, hold body in 1 hand and base of tentacles just above eyes in other hand. Pull gently to separate body and tentacles. Pull out and discard transparent "pen" from body; pull out and discard viscera and ink sac. Rinse body cavity. Pull off and discard any membrane covering body. Cut body crosswise into thin rings. Cut off tentacles just above eyes; discard eyes. Squeeze beak from base of tentacles; discard. Rinse tentacles. Set squid aside. Shell shrimp, leaving tail shells intact; set aside. Heat oil in a medium saucepan, add onion and cook until soft. Add garlic, tomatoes, soy sauce, ginger, chili and vinegar; cook 5 minutes. Stir squid rings and tentacles and shelled shrimp into sauce; cook, uncovered, 5 minutes or until squid is opaque and shrimp turn pink. Let seafood cool in sauce, then divide between 4 dishes and garnish with bell pepper strips. Makes 4 servings.

Avocado Crab Louis

Seafood Sauce, see below
8 oz. plain white crabmeat, flaked
12 medium avocados
Lemon juice
Lemon slices
Fresh chervil sprigs
Brown bread and butter (in pinwheels, if
   desired)

Seafood Sauce:
1/4 cup mayonnaise
1 tablespoon ketchup
1/2 teaspoon Worcestershire sauce
1/4 cup half and half
2 teaspoons lemon juice
Dash of dry sherry
Pinch of red (cayenne) pepper

To prepare Seafood Sauce, place all sauce ingredients in a bowl and blend well. Fold crabmeat into sauce. Pit, peel and slice avocados, then brush with lemon juice to prevent discoloration. Arrange avocado slices on 4 plates. Divide crabmeat mixture evenly among plates; garnish with lemon slices and chervil sprigs. Serve with brown bread and butter. Makes 4 servings.

Lamb with Spaghetti Squash

Red Pepper Dressing, see below
1 (about 1-1/2-lb.) spaghetti squash
About 1/2 cup frozen peas
1-1/4 to 1-1/2 lbs. thinly sliced rare roast
   lamb
Regular-strength beef or chicken broth
Salt and black pepper to taste
Fresh rosemary sprigs

Red Pepper Dressing:
2 small red bell peppers, roasted, skins and
   seeds removed
2 teaspoons sherry vinegar
6 tablespoons virgin olive oil
Salt and black pepper to taste

To prepare dressing, combine bell peppers, vinegar and oil in a blender; process until smooth. Season with salt and pepper and set aside. Cut squash in half lengthwise and remove seeds. Place squash, cut side down, in a large saucepan and add enough water to come halfway up sides of pan. Bring to a boil; reduce heat, cover and simmer 15 to 20 minutes or until squash is tender. Remove from pan; scoop flesh from shells with a fork and place in a colander to drain. Also cook peas in a little boiling water 2 to 3 minutes; drain. Place lamb slices in a large skillet, add a little broth and heat just until meat is warmed through. Season drained squash with salt and pepper; divide among 6 dinner plates. Arrange lamb on plates. Spoon some of Red Pepper Dressing over salads; offer remaining dressing separately. Garnish each plate with a spoonful of peas and a few rosemary sprigs. Makes 6 main-course servings.

Oriental Chicken Salad

8 radishes, cut into roses or fans
2 whole chicken breasts, cooked, skinned, boned
About 3 cups fresh bean sprouts
4 oz. fresh button mushrooms, stems trimmed, sliced
1 yellow bell pepper, seeded, diced
3 green onions, chopped
2 carrots, cut into thin julienne strips
1/2 quantity vinaigrette dressing
1 tablespoon sesame seeds, toasted

Place radishes in a bowl of ice water to make them open. Meanwhile, shred chicken and place in a bowl with bean sprouts, mushrooms, bell pepper, green onions and carrots. Stir together. Pour dressing over salad; toss to mix. Transfer salad to a serving dish; sprinkle with sesame seeds and garnish with radishes. Makes 4 servings.

Coronation Chicken

1 (4-lb.) broiler-fryer chicken, poached or boiled, cooled
Curry Mayonnaise, see below
Paprika
1 carrot, sliced, cut into flowers
1 celery stalk, cut into thin strips

Curry Mayonnaise:
1/4 cup mayonnaise
2 tablespoons lemon juice
2 tablespoons half and half
5 tablespoons plain yogurt
1 teaspoon tomato paste
1 teaspoon curry paste (or use curry powder to taste)
2 tablespoons mango chutney

Remove and discard skin and bones from chicken. Cut meat into neat, bite-size pieces and place on a platter. To prepare Curry Mayonnaise, place all ingredients in a blender and process until smooth. Pour Curry Mayonnaise over chicken. Dust with paprika. Garnish with carrot flowers and celery strips and serve. Makes 6 servings.

Lake Trout Salad

2 large lake trout, cleaned
Salt and black pepper to taste
Sunflower oil
4 carrots
2 zucchini
1 (6-inch) length cucumber
About 1 cup alfalfa sprouts
Vinaigrette Dressing
1 tablespoon chopped fresh tarragon
1 head Bibb lettuce
Nasturtium blossoms or watercress sprigs

Sprinkle trout with salt and pepper; brush with a little oil. Arrange on a broiler pan; broil, turning once, until opaque throughout. Let cool. Remove skin and bones; break flesh into neat pieces. Set aside. Peel carrots; then use a vegetable peeler to cut them into thin, broad ribbons (discard centers of carrots). Place carrot strips in a bowl. Cut zucchini diagonally into thin slices. Cook slices in boiling water 1 minute. Drain; add to carrots. Score sides of cucumber deeply with a fork or cut strips of peel from sides with a vegetable peeler. Cut cucumber in half lengthwise, then slice. Add cucumber and alfalfa sprouts to carrots and zucchini in bowl. Stir together Vinaigrette Dressing and tarragon; pour over vegetables and toss. Add trout and toss gently. Line 4 plates with lettuce; divide salad among plates. Garnish with nasturtium blossoms or watercress. Makes 4 servings.

German Sausage Salad

2 small (7-oz.) fully cooked German
   sausages, such as bierwurst or Bavarian
   ham sausage
1/2 head Bibb or iceberg lettuce, shredded
1 red bell pepper, seeded, diced
1 green bell pepper, seeded, diced
1 large head Belgian endive, sliced
1/2 cucumber, diced
Vinaigrette Dressing
1 teaspoon poppy seeds

Remove casings from sausages; dice sausages. Put lettuce in bottom of a glass salad bowl; scatter half the diced sausage over it. Top evenly with red and green bell peppers, then sprinkle on remaining diced sausage. Top with endive and cucumber; pour Vinaigrette Dressing over salad. Sprinkle with poppy seeds. Makes about 3 servings.

Fondue Bourguignonne

2 lbs. beef tenderloin

Tomato Sauce:
1 tablespoon vegetable oil
2 shallots, finely chopped
1 garlic clove, crushed
1 (14-oz.) can crushed tomatoes
2 tablespoons tomato paste
Salt and pepper
1 tablespoon chopped parsley

To make Tomato Sauce, heat oil in a medium-size saucepan, add shallots and cook slowly until soft.

Stir in garlic, tomatoes with their juice and tomato paste. Season with salt and pepper then bring to a boil. Reduce heat and simmer uncovered about 30 minutes or until sauce has thickened. Stir in parsley and serve hot or cold.

Cut beef tenderloin in 1-inch cubes and place in a serving dish. Each person spears a cube of meat with a fondue fork and puts the meat in the hot oil to deep-fry. The meat cube is cooked according to the individual's taste. Makes about 4 to 6 servings.

Bacon Bundles

12 slices (8 oz.) bacon
8 oz. chicken livers

Deviled Sauce:
1 tablespoon butter
1 shallot
1 tablespoon all-purpose flour
2/3 cup chicken broth
4 medium-size tomatoes, skinned, chopped
1 tablespoon tomato paste
2 teaspoons sugar
1 tablespoon red-wine vinegar
1 tablespoon Worcestershire sauce
1/2 teaspoon paprika
Dash cayenne pepper

Cut bacon slices in half. Trim chicken livers and cut in bite-size pieces.

Wrap bacon around chicken livers and spear on bamboo skewers; place on a serving plate.

To make Deviled Sauce, melt butter in a medium-size saucepan, add shallot and cook until soft. Stir in flour, then add remaining ingredients. Simmer 15 minutes; strain through a sieve. Serve hot. Makes about 4 servings.

Veal Milanese

1-1/2 lbs. cubed veal loin, leg or fillet
6 tablespoons all-purpose flour seasoned with
   salt and pepper
3 eggs, lightly beaten
2 teaspoons finely grated lemon peel
1-1/2 cups dry bread crumbs

Italian Sauce:
2 tablespoons olive oil
1 medium-size onion, finely chopped
1 to 2 garlic cloves, crushed
1-1/2 lbs. tomatoes, skinned, chopped
5 tablespoons dry white wine
1 tablespoon chopped fresh basil

Toss veal in seasoned flour, dip in beaten egg
and coat in mixture of bread crumbs and lemon
peel. Place on a serving plate.

To make Italian Sauce, heat oil in a medium-
size saucepan. Add onion and garlic and cook
over low heat until soft. Add tomatoes and
wine. Season with salt and pepper; simmer 30
minutes.

Process sauce in a blender or food processor
until smooth, or press through a sieve. Stir in
basil and reheat sauce before serving. Makes 4
to 6 servings.

Spicy Chicken Fondue

6 chicken breasts, boned, skinned
1/4 cup vegetable oil
2 teaspoons paprika
1/2 teaspoon chili powder

Curry Sauce:
1 medium-size onion, chopped
2 teaspoons curry powder
1 tablespoon all-purpose flour
1-1/4 cups milk
2 tablespoons mango chutney

Cut chicken in 3/4-inch pieces. Mix oil, paprika
and chili powder together; stir in chicken.

To make Curry Sauce, heat 1 tablespoon vegetable oil in small saucepan, add onion and cook
until soft. Stir in curry powder and cook 2
minutes; blend in flour.

Gradually stir in milk allowing mixture to slowly come to a boil. Continue cooking until sauce
thickens. Simmer 5 minutes then add chutney
and salt and pepper to taste. Serve hot. Makes 6
servings.

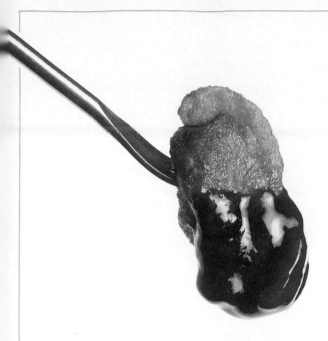

Fruity Duck Fondue

1-1/2 lbs. duck breast fillets
2 tablespoons all-purpose flour seasoned with salt, pepper and 1 teaspoon five spice powder

Marmalade Sauce:
1 tablespoon brown sugar
2/3 cup orange juice
1/4 cup orange marmalade
3 tablespoons lemon juice
1/4 cup raisins, chopped

Wine & Cherry Sauce:
1 tablespoon sugar
1 (16-oz.) can black cherries, drained, pitted
1/3 cup red wine
Pinch allspice

Cut duck in pieces 3/4 inch wide. Coat in seasoned flour.

To make Marmalade Sauce, simmer brown sugar, orange juice, marmalade, lemon juice and raisins in a small saucepan 5 minutes.

To make Wine & Cherry Sauce, simmer sugar, cherries, wine and allspice in a small saucepan 15 minutes. Press through a sieve; serve sauce warm. Makes about 4 servings.

Surprise Meatball Fondue

1-1/2 lbs. lean ground beef
1 tablespoon finely chopped onion
1/2 cup fresh whole-wheat bread crumbs
4 oz. Cheddar cheese, diced

Barbecue Sauce:
1 tablespoon tomato paste
1 tablespoon red-wine vinegar
2 tablespoons honey
2 teaspoons dry mustard
1 tablespoon Worcestershire sauce
1-1/4 cups chicken broth
2 teaspoons cornstarch
1/2 cup orange juice

In a bowl mix ground beef, onion and bread crumbs. Add salt and pepper to taste.

Shape meat mixture into 36 even-size balls. Flatten each ball slightly, place a piece of cheese in the middle and mold the meat around, sealing it well.

To make Barbecue Sauce, put tomato paste, vinegar, honey, dry mustard, Worcestershire sauce and broth in a small saucepan and simmer 10 minutes. Blend cornstarch with orange juice; stir into sauce and simmer 1 minute. Makes 4 to 6 servings.

Lamb Meatball Fondue

1-1/4 lbs. ground lamb
3 green onions, finely chopped
1 cup fresh bread crumbs
2 tablespoons chopped parsley

Mushroom Sauce:
1/4 cup butter
1/3 lb. mushrooms, finely chopped
2 tablespoons flour
1-1/4 cups milk
1 tablespoon dry sherry

Mix together all ingredients for lamb meatballs. Season with salt and pepper to taste.

With wet hands shape mixture into walnut-size balls and place on a serving plate.

To make Mushroom Sauce, melt butter in a small saucepan, add mushrooms and sauté over low heat 5 minutes. Stir in flour then slowly add milk. Simmer for 5 minutes longer; add sherry. Serve warm. Makes about 6 servings.

Crispy Pork Bites

1 pound very lean pork, finely ground
1 small onion, finely chopped
1/3 cup (8-oz.) pkg. cream cheese, room temperature
1 tablespoon chopped parsley
1 teaspoon prepared mustard
1/2 cup fresh bread crumbs
2 eggs, lightly beaten
3/4 cup dry bread crumbs

Chutney Sauce:
Tomato Sauce, page 71
2 tablespoons mango chutney

Put sausage and onion in a medium-size skillet and cook until sausage is lightly browned and crumbly.

Spoon into a medium-size bowl and add cream cheese, parsley, mustard and fresh bread crumbs; mix. Shape into small balls trying to make the surface smooth. Dip in beaten egg then roll in dry bread crumbs until evenly coated. Chill until ready to cook in hot oil.

To make Chutney Sauce, put Tomato Sauce in a medium-size saucepan and stir in chutney; heat through. Serve warm. Makes about 4 servings.

Middle-Eastern Lamb Fondue

1-1/2 lbs. boneless lamb

Marinade:
3 tablespoons olive oil
1 tablespoon lemon juice
1 garlic clove, crushed
1 tablespoon chopped fresh mint
1 teaspoon ground cinnamon
Salt and pepper

Apricot Sauce:
1 tablespoon vegetable oil
1 shallot, finely chopped
1 (16-oz.) can apricots in natural juice
1 tablespoon chopped parsley

Cut lamb in bite-size cubes. Mix marinade ingredients together, pour over lamb and marinate at least 2 hours, but preferably overnight.

To make Apricot Sauce, heat vegetable oil in a medium-size saucepan, add shallot and cook over low heat until soft. Add apricots and their juice and simmer 5 minutes.

Puree sauce in either a blender or food processor. Pour puree back into saucepan, stir in parsley and reheat before serving. Makes 4 to 6 servings.

Mexican Beef Fondue

2 lbs. beef tenderloin or sirloin

Mexican Sauce:
1 tablespoon vegetable oil
1/4 cup finely chopped yellow onion
1 garlic clove
1 (16-oz.) can peeled tomatoes
2 tablespoons tomato paste
1/2 teaspoon chili powder
1 green chili, finely chopped
Salt and pepper

Cut meat in 1-inch cubes and put on a serving plate.

To make Mexican Sauce, heat vegetable oil in a medium-size saucepan, add onion and garlic and cook gently until softened. Stir in tomatoes and their juice, tomato paste and chili powder. Simmer uncovered 10 minutes.

Remove sauce from heat and puree in a blender or food processor until smooth, or press through a sieve to give a smooth sauce. Return to heat, add chopped green chili and simmer 15 minutes. Season with salt and pepper to taste. Makes 4 to 6 servings.

Pork Saté

2 lbs. lean boneless pork
1/2 teaspoon chili powder
1 teaspoon ground coriander
1/2 teaspoon turmeric
1 tablespoon vegetable oil
1 tablespoon soy sauce
1/2 teaspoon salt

Peanut-Chili Sauce:
2/3 cup shredded coconut
1-1/4 cups boiling water
5 tablespoons crunchy peanut butter
2 teaspoons sugar
1 green chili, finely chopped
1 teaspoon lemon juice
1 garlic clove, crushed

Cut pork in 3/4-inch cubes.

In a large bowl mix together spices, vegetable oil, soy sauce and salt to make a paste; add pork. With wet hands, knead mixture into pork. Cover bowl and leave at least 2 hours.

To make Peanut-Chili Sauce, put coconut in a medium-size bowl and pour boiling water over. Let stand 15 minutes. Pour through a sieve into a medium-size bowl pressing the liquid through the sieve; discard coconut. Pour liquid into a saucepan. Add remaining ingredients to coconut liquid and mix well. Cook over low heat, stirring until sauce boils. Serve hot. Makes about 6 servings.

Teriyaki Fondue

2 lbs. lean beef tenderloin or sirloin
1 tablespoon brown sugar
1/2 cup soy sauce
6 tablespoons dry sherry
2 garlic cloves, crushed
1 teaspoon ground ginger

Bean Sprout Salad:
1 small head Chinese cabbage
8 oz. bean sprouts, roots trimmed
1 red bell pepper, finely sliced
6 green onions, shredded
6 tablespoons sunflower oil
1 tablespoon wine vinegar

Cut meat in thin strips 1/2 inch wide and 4 inches long.

Put 1 teaspoon brown sugar and 2 tablespoons soy sauce in a small bowl and set aside. In a large bowl combine remaining brown sugar and soy sauce with sherry, garlic and ginger; add meat and marinate 1 hour. Spear meat on bamboo skewers.

To prepare salad, shred Chinese cabbage and put in a salad bowl with bean sprouts, red bell pepper and green onions. Add sunflower oil to reserved sugar and soy sauce mixture and beat in vinegar. Pour over salad and toss together. Makes about 4 to 6 servings.

ACCOMPANIMENTS

ACCOMPANIMENTS

COOL AVOCADO DIP:
1 medium-size avocado
2 teaspoons lemon juice
2/3 cup sour cream
1 teaspoon grated onion
Salt and pepper

To make Cool Avocado Dip, cut avocado in half, discard seed and scoop flesh into a bowl. Mash with lemon juice until smooth then stir in sour cream, onion, salt and pepper. Makes about 1-1/2 cups.

CUCUMBER & YOGURT SAUCE:
2 oz. Neufchâtel cheese
2/3 cup plain low-fat yogurt
2/3 cup peeled, finely diced cucumber
2 teaspoons lemon juice
Salt and pepper

To make Cucumber & Yogurt Sauce, beat cheese and yogurt together until smooth. Blend in cucumber, lemon juice, salt and pepper. Makes about 2 cups.

ANCHOVY MAYONNAISE:
1 (1-1/2-oz.) can anchovies, drained
6 tablespoons mayonnaise
2 tablespoons half and half
2 tablespoons olive oil
2 teaspoons tomato paste

To make Anchovy Mayonnaise, place all ingredients in a blender or food processor and process until smooth. Makes about 1 cup.

SPICY ORIENTAL SAUCE:
2 tablespoons soy sauce
1-1/2 tablespoons lemon juice
2 green chili peppers, chopped
1 garlic clove, crushed
2 teaspoons sesame oil

To make Spicy Oriental Sauce, put all ingredients in a small bowl and mix together. Makes about 1/2 cup.

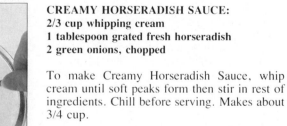

CREAMY HORSERADISH SAUCE:
2/3 cup whipping cream
1 tablespoon grated fresh horseradish
2 green onions, chopped

To make Creamy Horseradish Sauce, whip cream until soft peaks form then stir in rest of ingredients. Chill before serving. Makes about 3/4 cup.

MUSTARD SAUCE:
1 tablespoon Dijon mustard
2/3 cup sour cream
3 tablespoons mayonnaise
Salt and pepper

To make Mustard Sauce, put mustard, sour cream and mayonnaise in a small bowl and mix together until smooth. Season with salt and pepper. Makes about 1 cup.

Coeurs à la Créme

1 cup ricotta or cottage cheese
1 tablespoon plus 2 teaspoons superfine sugar
1 teaspoon lemon juice
1-1/4 cups whipping cream
2 egg whites
Fresh fruit and whipped cream, to serve, if
**   desired**

Line 4 heart-shaped molds with muslin. Press cheese through sieve into a bowl. Stir in sugar and lemon juice

In a separate bowl, whip cream until stiff. Stir into cheese mixture. Whisk egg whites until stiff, then fold into the cheese mixture.

Spoon cheese mixture into the molds, place on a plate overnight to drain. To serve, un-mold onto individual plates and gently remove the muslin. Serve hearts with fresh fruit and whipped cream, if desired.

Makes 4 to 6 servings.

Orange Caramel Cream

1/2 cup granulated sugar
3 tablespoons water
3 eggs
2 tablespoons plus 2 teaspoons superfine sugar
1-1/4 cups milk
1 tablespoon orange flower water
1 orange
Fresh herbs to decorate, if desired

Preheat oven to 350F (175C). Warm 4 china ramekin dishes or 4 dariole molds. In a sauce-pan, combine granulated sugar and water and cook over low heat, stirring to dissolve sugar. Increase heat and boil steadily, without stirring, to a rich brown caramel.

Divide caramel among dishes or molds and tip to cover bottom and sides with caramel. Set aside. In a bowl, beat eggs and superfine sugar. In a saucepan, heat milk until almost boiling, then pour over egg mixture, beating constantly. Stir in orange flower water.

Strain mixture into dishes or molds. Grate orange peel finely and section orange; re-serve orange sections. Divide orange peel among dishes and stir in. Place dishes in a roasting pan. Pour in boiling water to come halfway up sides, then bake about 20 minutes, until set. Cool in dishes and chill until needed. Turn out onto serving plates and decorate with reserved orange sections and fresh herbs, if desired.

Makes 4 servings.

NOTE: A dariole mold is a small cylindrical mold used for cooking pastries or vegetables.

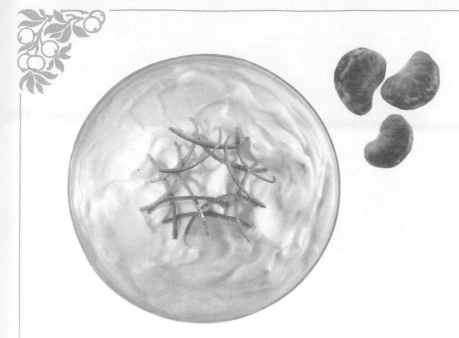

Tangerine Syllabub

Grated peel and juice of 3 tangerines
Grated peel and juice of 1 lemon
1/3 cup superfine sugar
1/3 cup cream sherry
1-1/4 cups whipping cream
Additional grated peel to decorate, if desired

In a bowl, combine tangerine and lemon peels and juices, sugar and sherry. Chill at least 1 hour to infuse.

In a large bowl, whip cream while gradually pouring in tangerine mixture. Whip until mixture is thick enough to form soft peaks.

Pour mixture into a glass serving bowl or individual dessert dishes and chill at least 2 hours before serving. Decorate with additional grated peel, if desired.

Makes 4 to 6 servings.

NOTE: Use a sharp grater to grate tangerine peel, otherwise peel tends to tear.
Warm citrus fruits slightly before squeezing and they will yield more juice.

Banana Brûlée

2-1/2 cups whipping cream
3 large bananas
Juice of 1 small lemon
1/4 cup superfine sugar
1/2 cup granulated sugar
1 tablespoon water

In a large bowl, whip cream until thick. Slice bananas thinly into a separate bowl and toss in lemon juice.

Fold bananas and superfine sugar into whipped cream. Spoon mixture into a serving dish and chill.

In a small saucepan, combine granulated sugar and water. Cook over low heat until sugar dissolves, do not stir. When sugar has dissolved increase heat and boil syrup to a rich brown caramel. Immediately pour caramel in a thin stream over banana cream mixture and chill until caramel hardens. Serve within 1 to 2 hours.

Makes 6 servings.

Coffee Bombe

Charlotte Russe

8 ready-made Meringues
3 eggs, separated
3/4 cup superfine sugar
1-1/3 cups cold strong coffee
2 cups whipping cream
Whipped cream and chocolate coffee beans to
**   decorate, if desired**

Lightly oil a 4-cup bombe mold. In a large bowl, beat egg yolks and sugar until thick and mousse-like. Gently stir in coffee. In a separate bowl, whip cream lightly. Crush meringues.

Fold cream and meringues into coffee mixture. In a medium-size bowl, whisk egg whites until stiff and fold 1 tablespoon into coffee mixture. Carefully fold coffee mixture into egg whites. Pour into oiled mold and freeze until firm.

One hour before serving, place bombe in refrigerator to soften slightly. Turn out bombe onto a serving dish and decorate with whipped cream and chocolate coffee beans, if desired.

Makes 8 servings.

Note: To remove bombe, immerse a tea towel in very hot water, wring out and wrap around mold. Invert onto a serving plate and lift off mold.

16 ladyfingers
1 (1/4-oz.) envelope unflavored gelatin
**   (1 tablespoon)**
3 tablespoons water
4 egg yolks
1/3 cup superfine sugar
2-1/2 cups whipping cream
1 vanilla bean, split open
1-1/4 cups dairy sour cream
Additional whipped cream and 1-1/4 cups fresh
**   raspberries to decorate**

Line bottom of a 4-1/4-cup charlotte mold with waxed paper. Stand ladyfingers, pressing against each other, around sides of mold and trim to fit.

In a small bowl, sprinkle gelatin over water and let stand 2 to 3 minutes, until softened. In a bowl, whisk egg yolks and sugar until thick and mousse-like. In a saucepan, place 1-1/2 cups of whipping cream and vanilla bean and bring almost to a boil. Strain over egg mixture, stirring well. Pour back into saucepan and stir over low heat until mixture has thickened slightly; do not boil.

Strain into a clean bowl and add gelatin. Stir until dissolved. Cool, then set bowl in a larger bowl of iced water and stir until mixture thickens. Whip remaining cream with sour cream and fold into mixture. Pour into prepared mold, cover with plastic wrap and chill overnight. To serve, turn out onto a serving plate. Remove waxed paper and decorate with additional whipped cream and raspberries. Tie ribbon around pudding.

Makes 6 to 8 servings.

Oeufs à la Neige

4 eggs, separated
1/2 teaspoon cornstarch
1/3 cup superfine sugar
1/2 cup milk
1-1/4 cups half and half
1 vanilla bean
1 tablespoon orange flower water
1 tablespoon toasted whole almonds and orange
    peel strips to decorate, if desired

In a bowl, cream egg yolks, cornstarch and 1/2 of sugar. In a saucepan, scald milk, half and half and vanilla bean.

Pour hot milk over egg yolks, whisking constantly. Pour egg mixture back into pan; set over a pan of simmering water and cook gently, stirring constantly, until consistency of thick cream. Cool, remove vanilla bean and stir in orange flower water. In a large bowl, whisk egg whites until stiff, add remaining sugar and whisk again.

Fill a large pan with water and bring to simmering point. Drop spoonfuls of meringue mixture, a few at a time, into water and poach 5 minutes, carefully turning once. Drain on paper towels and cool. Pour custard into a glass serving bowl and arrange meringue puffs on top. Decorate with toasted almonds and orange peel strips, if desired.

Makes 4 servings.

Red Berry Soufflé

2 tablespoons butter
1/2 cup plus 1 tablespoon superfine sugar
1-3/4 cups mixed red berries, thawed if frozen
1 tablespoon strawberry liqueur or crème de
    cassis
5 egg whites
Powdered sugar to serve

Preheat oven to 350F (175C). Butter a 4-cup soufflé dish, then dust with 1 tablespoon of superfine sugar.

In a blender or food processor, process remaining superfine sugar, berries and liqueur to a puree. Pour into a bowl. In a separate bowl, whisk egg whites until stiff but not dry. Fold 1 tablespoon of whipped egg whites into puree. Pour puree onto whipped egg whites and, using a metal spoon, carefully fold in.

Spoon mixture into prepared soufflé dish. Place dish on a baking sheet and bake 25 to 30 minutes, until risen and just set. Dust with powdered sugar and serve immediately.

Makes 6 servings.

NOTE: If desired, spoon mixture into 6 individual soufflé dishes and bake 15 to 20 minutes.

Framboise Zabaglione

4 egg yolks
3/4 cup plus 2 tablespoons framboise liqueur
1 tablespoon plus 2 teaspoons superfine sugar
Fresh strawberries and leaves to garnish, if desired
Langue de chats cookies to serve

Combine egg yolks, liqueur and sugar in a double boiler or a bowl set over a pan of simmering water.

Whisk mixture over medium heat until very thick and mousse-like, about 20 minutes.

Pour mixture into serving dishes. Garnish with strawberries and leaves, if desired, and serve immediately with cookies.

Makes 4 servings.

NOTE: It is important to use a whisk for this recipe. An electric mixer increases the volume of the eggs too quickly so that they do not have a chance to cook. The mixture will then collapse when poured into the serving dishes.

Chocolate Trifle

3-1/2 ounces semisweet chocolate
2 tablespoons rum
2 tablespoons water
4 egg yolks
1 tablespoon superfine sugar
3 cups whipping cream
8 ounces plain or trifle sponge cakes
1/2 cup apricot jam
12 ounces mixed fruit such as grapes, ripe pears and bananas
Grated semisweet chocolate to decorate, if desired

In top of a double boiler or a bowl set over a saucepan of simmering water, melt chocolate with rum and water.

In a large bowl, whisk egg yolks and sugar until light and fluffy. In a saucepan, bring whipping cream almost to boiling point. Whisk into egg yolk mixture with melted chocolate mixture. Return mixture to saucepan and whisk over a very low heat until chocolate is incorporated and mixture has thickened slightly. Slice sponge cakes in half. In a small saucepan warm jam slightly and brush over sponge cakes.

Place sponge cakes in individual serving dishes. Half and seed grapes; peel, core and finely slice pears and slice bananas. Sprinkle fruit over sponge cakes. Lightly whip remaining cream. Spoon chocolate sauce over fruit and spread whipped cream over chocolate sauce. Decorate with grated chocolate, if desired. Chill until ready to serve.

Makes 6 servings.

White & Dark Chocolate Terrine

White Chocolate Mousse:
9 ounces white chocolate
1/2 (1/4-oz.) envelope unflavored gelatin
    (1-1/2 teaspoons)
5 tablespoons water
1 tablespoon light corn syrup
2 egg yolks
2/3 cup whipping cream
2/3 cup dairy sour cream

Dark Chocolate Mousse:
6 ounces semisweet chocolate
1/4 cup strong coffee
2/3 (1/4-oz.) envelope unflavored gelatin
    (2 teaspoons)
3 tablespoons water
8 tablespoons butter, cubed
2 egg yolks
1-1/4 cups whipping cream

Whipped cream and grated semisweet
    chocolate to decorate, if desired

Line an 8" x 4" loaf pan with plastic wrap to overlap edges. To prepare white chocolate mousse, break white chocolate in small pieces and set aside. In a small bowl, sprinkle gelatin over 2 tablespoons of water and let stand 2 to 3 minutes, until softened. In a saucepan, combine remaining water and corn syrup and bring to boil. Remove from heat and stir in gelatin until dissolved. Add chocolate pieces and beat until chocolate is melted and mixture is smooth.

Beat in egg yolks, 1 at a time. In a bowl, whip whipping cream and sour cream lightly and fold into chocolate mixture. Pour into prepared loaf pan and refrigerate until set.

To prepare dark chocolate mousse, in top of a double boiler or bowl set over a pan of simmering water, melt chocolate with coffee. In a small bowl, sprinkle gelatin over water and let stand 2 to 3 minutes, until softened. Set bowl of gelatin in a saucepan of hot water and stir until dissolved. Stir gelatin and butter into chocolate mixture and beat until butter has melted and mixture is smooth. Cool, then beat in egg yolks. In a bowl, whip cream lightly and fold into chocolate mixture.

Pour dark chocolate mixture over set white chocolate mousse. Refrigerate until set, then cover with overlapping plastic wrap and refrigerate overnight.

To serve, unfold plastic wrap from top and turn out onto a serving dish. Carefully peel off plastic wrap. Decorate with whipped cream and grated chocolate, if desired, and cut in slices.

Makes 8 to 10 servings.

Molded Chocolate Pudding

Rich Chocolate Log

9 ounces semisweet chocolate
1/4 cup plus 1 tablespoon strong coffee
12 tablespoons unsalted butter, diced
3/4 cup superfine sugar
4 large eggs, beaten
1-1/2 cups whipping cream
Tiny edible flowers to decorate, if desired

Preheat oven to 350F (175C). Line a 4-cup bowl or soufflé dish with a double thickness of foil.

1 (14-oz.) can sweetened condensed milk
3 ounces semisweet chocolate
3 tablespoons butter
1 pound plain sponge cake
2/3 cup glacé cherries, halved
1/2 cup walnuts, chopped
3 tablespoons chopped pitted dates

Chocolate Fudge Icing:
3 tablespoons butter
1/4 cup superfine sugar
2 tablespoons water
1/2 cup powdered sugar
1/4 cup unsweetened cocoa powder

In top of a double boiler or bowl set over a pan of simmering water, melt chocolate with coffee. Gradually beat in butter and sugar and heat until mixture is hot and butter melts. Remove from heat and gradually whisk in eggs. Strain mixture into prepared dish, cover with foil and place in a roasting pan. Add enough boiling water to pan to come halfway up dish. Bake 1 hour, until top has a thick crust. Cool, then refrigerate.

Glacé cherries, cut in strips, and walnut halves to garnish, if desired

In a saucepan, combine milk, chocolate and butter. Stir over low heat until chocolate and butter have melted and ingredients are well combined. Remove from heat. In a blender or food processor fitted with the metal blade, process cake to crumbs. Stir crumbs into chocolate mixture. Stir in cherries, walnuts and dates. Spoon mixture onto a large piece of waxed paper and form in a log shape. Roll up in waxed paper. Chill overnight.

To serve, unmold pudding onto a serving dish and carefully peel away foil; pudding is rich and sticky. In a bowl, whip cream until stiff, then cover pudding with 2/3 of whipped cream. Using a pastry bag fitted with a star nozzle, pipe remaining whipped cream in rosettes around top and bottom of pudding. Decorate with flowers, if desired.

Makes 6 to 8 servings.

Two hours before serving, unwrap log and place on a serving dish. To prepare icing, in a saucepan, combine butter, superfine sugar and water. Bring to a boil. Sift powdered sugar and cocoa into pan and beat well. Cool until fudgy, then spread over roll. Mark lines along roll with a fork. Garnish with glacé sherry strips and walnut halves, if desired.

Makes 8 to 10 servings.

Pineapple Alaska

1 large ripe pineapple with leaves
1 to 2 tablespoons kirsch
1 quart vanilla ice cream
3 egg whites
3/4 cup plus 1 tablespoon superfine sugar

Cut pineapple in half lengthwise. Using a grapefruit knife, cut out pulp. Discard core, then cut pulp in chunks and place in a bowl. Sprinkle with kirsch, cover with plastic wrap and chill pulp and pineapple shells overnight.

Place pineapple chunks in shells and pack ice cream on top. Freeze about 2 hours, until very firm. Preheat oven to 400F (205C). Whisk egg whites in a bowl until stiff. Whisk in 1/4 cup plus 2 tablespoons of sugar, then whisk 1 minute more. Fold in 1/4 cup plus 2 tablespoons of sugar.

Pile meringue over ice cream, completely covering ice cream. Make small peaks in meringue with a flat-bladed knife. Place pineapple shells on a baking sheet and sprinkle with remaining sugar. Bake about 8 minutes, until meringue is set and brown. Serve immediately.

Makes 6 servings.

VARIATION: Prepare this dessert using a fruit sorbet instead of vanilla ice cream.

Mango Mousse

1 (16-oz.) can mangoes
Juice of 1/2 lemon
1 to 2 tablespoons superfine sugar
1 (1/4-oz.) envelope unflavored gelatin
   (1 tablespoon)
1/4 cup plus 1 tablespoon water
1-1/4 cups whipping cream
Fresh mango slices and lemon peel strips to
   decorate

Drain mangoes well. In a blender or food processor fitted with the metal blade, process mangoes and lemon juice to a puree. Sweeten to taste with sugar.

In a small bowl, sprinkle gelatin over water and let stand 2 to 3 minutes, until softened. Set bowl of gelatin in a saucepan of hot water and stir until dissolved. Stir gelatin into puree, then chill until almost set. In a bowl, whip cream lightly and gently fold into mango mixture.

Pour mixture into a glass serving bowl or individual serving dishes and refrigerate until set. Decorate with fresh mango slices and lemon peel strips to serve.

Makes 4 servings.

NOTE: When folding whipped cream and/or egg whites into gelatin mixture, the gelatin mixture must be almost set. If folded in too soon, the mixture will separate with the gelatin on bottom and froth on top.

Frozen Loganberry Soufflé

Lychee Sorbet

1 pound loganberries or raspberries
Lemon juice to taste
2/3 cup superfine sugar
1/2 cup water
3 egg whites
1-3/4 cups whipping cream
Fresh raspberries and mint leaves to garnish, if
** desired**

In a blender or food processor fitted with the metal blade, process berries to a puree, then sieve to remove seeds. Flavor with lemon juice.

2 (16-oz.) cans lychees in syrup
Grated peel and juice of 1 lemon
2 egg whites
Mint leaves to garnish, if desired

Drain lychees, reserving 1-1/4 cups of syrup. In a blender or food processor fitted with the metal blade, process lychees, syrup and lemon juice to a puree.

In a small saucepan, combine sugar and water. Cook over low heat. When sugar dissolves, bring syrup to a boil and boil to 240F (115C). In a large bowl, whisk egg whites until stiff. Gradually pour in sugar syrup, whisking constantly. Continue whisking until meringue is firm and cool. In a bowl, whip cream lightly and fold into meringue mixture with fruit puree.

Stir in lemon peel, pour into a plastic container and freeze about 1 hour, until mixture is slushy.

Divide mixture among 6 ramekin dishes and freeze 2 to 3 hours. Transfer to refrigerator 30 minutes before serving. Garnish with fresh raspberries and mint leaves, if desired.

Makes 6 servings.

NOTE: For a special occasion, wrap foil around tops of small ramekin dishes so that foil extends 2 inches above rim. Keep in place with freezer tape. Fill dishes to come over the top, so when foil is removed, they look like risen soufflés.

In a large bowl, whisk egg whites until stiff. Fold in semifrozen lychee puree and combine thoroughly. Freeze until firm. To serve, scoop sorbet in balls and garnish with mint leaves, if desired.

Makes 4 to 6 servings.

NOTE: For a smoother texture, whisk sorbet about 1 hour after adding egg whites. Serve sorbet as soon as possible for the best flavor.

Tarte Francaise

13 ounces fresh or frozen puff pastry
1 egg yolk, beaten
1/4 cup plus 2 tablespoons apricot jam, sieved
2 tablespoons lemon juice
1-1/2 pounds mixed fresh fruit such as grapes, strawberries, raspberries and bananas
Additional strawberries and leaves to garnish, if desired

Thaw pastry, if frozen, and roll out to a 12" x 8" rectangle. Fold pastry in half. Cut a rectangle from folded edge 1-1/2 inches in from outside edges.

Unfold middle section and roll out to a 12" x 8" rectangle. Place on a baking sheet, dampen edges with water, then unfold frame and place carefully on top of pastry rectangle. Press edges of pastry together. Mark a pattern on frame and brush with beaten egg yolk. Prick center all over.

Preheat oven to 425F (220C). Chill pastry 10 minutes, then bake about 20 minutes, until golden-brown; cool. In a saucepan, heat jam and lemon juice gently until jam has melted. Halve and seed grapes. Leave strawberries and raspberries whole and peel and slice bananas. Brush bottom of tart lightly with jam and arrange prepared fruit in rows. Brush fruit with jam and garnish with additional strawberries and leaves, if desired. Serve as soon as possible.

Makes 6 servings.

Strawberry Mille-Feuille

13 ounces fresh or frozen puff pastry
1 pound strawberries
1-1/4 cups whipping cream
1 to 2 drops vanilla extract
Sugar to taste
1/4 cup plus 1 tablespoon red currant jelly
2 tablespoons water

Thaw pastry, if frozen. Preheat oven to 425F (220C). Roll out pastry to a thin rectangle and cut in 3 equal sections.

Place sections on baking sheets and prick all over with a fork. Bake 15 to 20 minutes, until golden-brown and crisp. Cool on a wire rack. When cold, trim edges with a very sharp knife to make even. Reserve trimmings. Cut 1/2 of strawberries in half, using even-sized ones. Slice remainder. In a bowl, whip cream until fairly stiff and flavor with vanilla and sugar. Fold sliced strawberries into whipped cream.

Place 1 pastry slice on a serving plate and spread with 1/2 of whipped cream mixture. Lay another slice on top and spread with remaining cream mixture. Top with remaining slice. In a small saucepan, heat jelly and water gently until jelly has dissolved. Brush top slice with jelly and arrange halved strawberries on top. Brush with remainder of jelly. Crush reserved pastry trimmings and press into sides of mille-feuille.

Makes 6 to 8 servings.

Victoria Sponge Cake

8 tablespoons margarine or butter, softened
1/2 cup superfine sugar
2 large eggs, beaten
1 cup self-rising flour
Milk, if necessary
Whipped cream and sliced strawberries and
    kiwifruit to serve
Additional strawberries and leaves to garnish,
    if desired

Preheat oven to 350F (175C). Grease 2 (8-inch) round cake pans.

In a bowl, cream margarine and sugar until light and fluffy. Beat eggs into creamed margarine and sugar, a little at a time. Sift flour into mixture and fold in, using a metal spoon. Mixture should be a soft dropping consistency; add a little milk, if necessary. Spoon into greased pan. Bake about 20 to 25 minutes, until golden and spongy to touch. Turn out and cool on a wire rack.

Spread 1/2 of whipped cream on top of 1 cake and arrange 1/2 of fruit on whipped cream. Top with remaining cake. Spread or pipe remaining whipped cream on top of cake and arrange remaining fruit on whipped cream. Garnish with additional strawberries and leaves, if desired.

Makes 6 servings.

VARIATION: Flavor with a few drops of vanilla extract or 1 tablespoon grated orange or lemon peel. Beat into mixture before adding flour.

Coffee-Brandy Cake

1 recipe Victoria Sponge Cake, see left
2 tablespoons brandy
1 tablespoon superfine sugar
1-1/4 cups hot strong coffee
1-1/4 cups whipping cream
1 tablespoon powdered sugar
1/2 cup sliced almonds, toasted

Preheat sponge cake as directed and bake in a 2-1/2-cup greased bowl. Cool in bowl.

When cake is cold, stir brandy and superfine sugar into hot coffee and pour over cake while still in bowl. Place a saucer over bowl and chill overnight.

About 2 hours before serving, run a knife around edges of cake, then turn out on a serving plate. In a bowl, whip cream and powdered sugar until very stiff and spread evenly over cake, covering completely; chill. Just before serving, stick toasted almonds into surface of whipped cream all over cake.

Makes 4 to 6 servings.

Variation: Using a pastry bag fitted with a star nozzle, pipe rosettes of whipped cream all over cake and decorate with sliced almonds, and tiny edible flowers.

Cherry Sponge Flans

1 recipe Victoria Sponge Cake, see page 88
1 pound fresh sweet dark cherries, pitted
1 tablespoon superfine sugar
1 teaspoon arrowroot
1 tablespoon water
1 tablespoon kirsch
1-1/4 cups whipping cream
Fresh sweet cherries and mint leaves to garnish, if desired

Preheat oven to 350F (175C). Grease 8 individual 4-inch pans, then dust with sugar and flour. Prepare sponge cake as directed. Divide among greased pans and bake 5 to 10 minutes, until golden and spongy to touch.

Cool in pans. In a saucepan, combine cherries and sugar. Cover and cook over low heat until juices run. Mix arrowroot and water to a smooth paste and stir into cherries. Bring to a boil, stirring constantly, then remove from heat; cool. Stir in kirsch.

To serve, place sponge cakes on individual serving plates. In a bowl, whip cream until stiff and spread over sponge cakes. Spoon cherries and sauce over whipped cream. Using a pastry bag fitted with a star nozzle, pipe a border of whipped cream around cherries. Garnish with fresh cherries and mint leaves, if desired, and serve immediately.

Makes 8 servings.

Chocolate & Chestnut Gâteau

12 tablespoons butter, softened
1/2 cup superfine sugar
6 ounces semisweet chocolate
3 tablespoons strong coffee
1 (14-oz.) can unsweetened chestnut puree
1-1/4 cups whipping cream

Oil an 8" x 4" loaf pan. In a bowl, cream butter and sugar until light and fluffy.

In top of a double boiler or bowl set over a pan of simmering water, melt chocolate with coffee. Add chestnut puree and melted chocolate to creamed butter and beat until smooth. Spoon mixture into oiled pan and level surface. Cover with foil and freeze 3 hours.

Turn out onto a serving plate. In a bowl, whip cream until stiff. Using a pastry bag fitted with a star nozzle, pipe rosettes of whipped cream on top. Let gâteau stand 30 minutes at room temperature to soften before serving.

Makes 6 to 8 servings.

Walnut & Butterscotch Gâteau

1 cup pitted dates, chopped
1 cup boiling water
8 tablespoons butter, softened
1 egg
1 cup superfine sugar
Few drops vanilla extract
1-1/2 cups all-purpose flour
1 teaspoon baking soda
1 teaspoon baking powder
1 teaspoon salt
1/2 cup walnuts, chopped

Butterscotch Icing:
2 tablespoons whipping cream
1 tablespoon butter
2 tablespoons light-brown sugar

Preheat oven to 350F (175C). Grease an 8" x 4" loaf pan. Place dates in a bowl and cover with boiling water; cool. In a bowl, cream butter, egg, sugar and vanilla until light and fluffy. Sift dry ingredients into mixture and fold in with dates and soaking liquid. Fold in chopped walnuts and pour into greased pan. Bake 1 to 1-1/2 hours, until spongy to touch. Turn out of pan.

To prepare icing, combine all ingredients in a small saucepan. Cook over medium heat, stirring constantly. Bring to a boil and pour over cake. Serve at once.

Makes 6 to 8 servings.

NOTE: To prevent dates sticking when chopping, dip the knife in hot water.

Hot Orange Cake

8 tablespoons butter, softened
1/2 cup superfine sugar
2 large eggs, separated
1 cup self-rising flour
Grated peel and juice of 3 small oranges
1 cup whipping cream
Powdered sugar and fresh orange sections to
    decorate

Preheat oven to 350F (175C). In a large bowl, cream butter and superfine sugar until light and fluffy. Beat egg yolks into mixture with 1 tablespoon of flour and grated peel and juice of 1 orange.

In a separate bowl, whisk egg whites until stiff but not dry; fold into creamed mixture with remaining flour. Spoon into a deep 8-inch nonstick cake pan. Bake 20 to 30 minutes, until golden-brown and springy to touch.

Meanwhile, in a bowl, whip cream and remaining orange juice and peel until stiff. Leave cake in pan 2 to 3 minutes, then turn out and cut in half crosswise. Working quickly, spread bottom with whipped cream and cover with top half of cake. Dust thickly with powdered sugar and arrange orange sections on top. Serve at once.

Makes 6 servings.

NOTE: The whipped cream will melt, so serve as quickly as possible.

Rum Truffle Cake

7 (1-oz.) squares semi-sweet chocolate
1/2 cup unsalted butter
1/4 cup dark rum
3 eggs, separated
1/2 cup superfine sugar
3/4 cup all-purpose flour
1/2 cup ground almonds

Filling & Icing:
7 (1-oz.) squares semi-sweet chocolate
1-1/4 cups whipping cream
1 tablespoon dark rum
2 (1-oz.) squares white chocolate, grated

Preheat oven to 350F (175C). Butter and flour a 2-1/2-inch deep .8-inch-round cake pan. Line bottom with a circle of waxed paper.

Place chocolate and butter in a bowl over hand-hot water. Stir occasionally until melted. Add rum and stir well.

Place egg yolks and sugar in a bowl over a saucepan of simmering water. Whisk until thick and pale. Remove bowl from saucepan. Continue to whisk until mixture leaves a trail when whisk has been lifted. Stir chocolate mixture into egg yolk mixture until evenly blended. In a small bowl, mix flour and ground almonds. Add to chocolate mixture; fold in carefully using a spatula.

In a bowl, whisk egg whites until stiff. Fold 1/3 at a time into chocolate mixture until all egg whites are incorporated. Pour mixture into prepared pan. Bake in oven 45 to 55 minutes or until firm to touch in center. Turn out of pan and cool on a wire rack.

To prepare filling, melt 4 squares of chocolate with 1/4 cup of whipping cream in a bowl set over hot water. Stir in rum until well blended. Let stand until cool. To prepare icing, whip 1/2 cup of whipping cream in a bowl until thick. Add 1/2 of rum-chocolate to whipped cream and fold in until smooth.

Cut cake in half. Sandwich together with chocolate icing and spread remainder over top and sides. Chill cake and remaining rum-chocolate mixture in bowl. Melt remaining chocolate with whipping cream in a bowl set over hot water. Stir until smooth and cool until thick. Spread chocolate mixture over cake to cover evenly. Shape rum-chocolate mixture into 16 truffles. Coat in grated white chocolate. Arrange truffles on top of cake and chill to set. Makes 10 servings.

Glacé Fruit Cake

Cake:
2-1/2 cups mixed glacé fruit, chopped
3/4 cup dried apricots, chopped
1 cup chopped pecans
Finely grated peel and juice 1 lemon
3 cups all-purpose flour
1 teaspoon baking powder
1-1/2 teaspoons ground mixed spice
1-2/3 cups ground almonds
1-3/4 cups superfine sugar
1-1/2 cups butter, softened
4 eggs

Topping:
1/4 cup apricot jam
2 teaspoons water
Mixed glacé fruit and nuts
Ribbon and holly sprigs to decorate

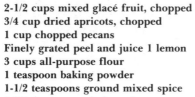

Preheat oven to 275F (135C). Line a 2-1/2-inch deep 8-inch-square cake pan or a 2-1/2-inch deep 9-inch-round pan with a double thickness of greased waxed paper, extending greased waxed paper above edge of pan. Place pan on baking sheet lined with a double thickness of waxed paper.

Combine glacé fruit, apricots, nuts and lemon peel and juice. Sift flour, baking powder and mixed spice into a bowl. Mix in ground almonds, sugar, butter and eggs, then beat 2 to 3 minutes or until smooth and glossy. Stir in mixed fruit and nuts.

Spoon mixture into prepared pan. Smooth top and bake 2-1/4 to 2-1/2 hours or until cake feels firm and springy. Cool in pan, then turn out and wrap in foil. In a saucepan, bring jam and water to a boil, stirring constantly, then sieve. Brush top of cake with jam. Arrange fruit and nuts over top and brush with remaining jam. Let stand until set. Decorate with ribbon and holly. Makes 30 servings.

Maraschino Fruit Ring

1 cup self-rising flour
3/4 cup light-brown sugar
1/2 cup butter, softened
3 eggs
1/2 cup pecans, chopped
1/2 cup dark raisins
1/2 cup red maraschino cherries, drained, sliced
1/2 cup green glacé cherries, drained, sliced
1/2 cup powdered sugar, sifted
2 tablespoons plus 2 teaspoons maraschino cherry syrup
6 red and 6 green maraschino cherries, sliced
Holly sprig to decorate

Preheat oven to 300F (150C). Lightly oil a 9-inch ring mold. In a bowl, combine flour, brown sugar, butter and eggs until well mixed, then beat 1 to 2 minutes or until smooth and glossy. Add pecans, raisins and cherries to mixture; stir until evenly mixed. Spoon mixture into oiled ring mold. Level top and bake in oven about 1 hour or until cake feels firm to touch. Test with a skewer; when skewer is inserted into center of cake, skewer should come out clean. Loosen edges of cake with a knife and cool in pan. Invert onto a wire rack.

In a bowl, combine powdered sugar and enough cherry syrup to make a consistency of thick cream. Spoon icing over cold cake. Arrange cherry slices in clusters around top of cake. Let stand until set. Decorate with holly sprig. Makes 10 servings.

Kastoberstorte

Spongecake Top & Bottom:
2 eggs
3 tablespoons sugar
2 tablespoons all-purpose flour
2 tablespoons cornstarch

Filling:
4 oz. cream cheese, softened
1/2 cup cottage cheese, sieved
2/3 cup plain yogurt
1/3 cup raisins
Finely grated peel and juice of 1 orange
2/3 cup whipping cream, whipped
1 tablespoon gelatin
2 tablespoons water
2 eggs
2 tablespoons honey

Garnish:
Powdered sugar

Preheat oven to 400F (205C). Grease 2 baking sheets and line with parchment paper. Trace a 9-inch circle on each sheet. To prepare spongecake bottom and top, beat eggs and sugar until they are thick and foamy and hold a ribbon when drawn over surface. Sift flour and cornstarch over egg mixture and fold in. Spoon spongecake mixture on baking sheets; spread beyond traced circles. Bake in preheated oven 12 to 15 minutes with oven door ajar 1/2-inch. Cool completely. To prepare filling, beat cream cheese, cottage cheese and yogurt in a large bowl until smooth. Stir in raisins and orange peel and juice. Fold in whipped cream. Combine gelatin and water in a small saucepan. Simmer until gelatin is completely dissolved; stir into cheese mixture. Beat eggs and honey until they are thick and foamy and hold a ribbon when drawn over surface; fold into cheese mixture. To assemble, trim spongecakes to a diameter of 9-inches. Place 1 spongecake in a 9-inch springform pan. Spoon filling over spongecake in pan. Refrigerate 2 to 3 hours or until set. Place remaining spongecake on filling. To garnish, dust with powdered sugar.

Makes 8 to 10 servings.

Tofu-Banana Cheesecake

Crust:
1/4 cup butter
1 cup crushed vanilla wafers

Filling:
12 oz. tofu, cut in 1/2-inch pieces
1-1/2 cups cottage cheese, sieved
2 ripe bananas, peeled, mashed
1 tablespoon honey
1 tablespoon all-purpose flour
Finely grated peel and juice of 1 lime

Garnish:
2 bananas
1/4 cup apricot jam
1 tablespoon lemon juice
Angelica pieces, cut in "leaves"

Preheat oven to 350F (175C). Grease an 8-inch springform pan. To prepare crust, melt butter in a small saucepan over low heat. Stir in crushed vanilla wafers. Press mixture in bottom of greased pan. Set aside. To prepare filling, beat tofu, cottage cheese, bananas, honey, flour and lime peel and juice until smooth. Spoon filling into prepared crust. Bake in preheated oven 45 minutes or until set. To garnish, slice bananas diagonally in ovals. Arrange slices around edge of cheesecake. Heat apricot jam and lemon juice in a small saucepan over low heat until mixture liquifies. Brush bananas with glaze. Arrange angelica "leaves" on banana slices.

Makes 8 to 10 servings.

Marbled Cheesecake

Crust:
1/4 cup butter
1-3/4 cups graham cracker crumbs

Filling:
1-1/2 lb. Neufchâtel cheese, softened
Scant 1/2 cup sugar
1 tablespoon all-purpose flour
3 eggs
1 teaspoon vanilla extract
3 oz. semisweet chocolate, broken in
  pieces

Preheat oven to 350F (175C). Grease an 8-inch springform pan. To prepare crust, melt butter in a small saucepan over low heat. Stir in graham cracker crumbs. Press mixture in bottom of greased pan. Set aside. To prepare filling, beat Neufchâtel cheese, sugar, flour, eggs and vanilla in a medium-size bowl until smooth. Spoon filling into prepared crust. Melt chocolate in top of a double boiler or a bowl set over a pan of simmering water. Pour melted chocolate in a thin stream over cheese mixture. Using handle of a teaspoon, swirl to combine 2 mixtures to achieve a marbled effect. Bake in preheated oven 45 minutes or until set. Cool before removing from pan.

Makes 8 to 10 servings.

Boston Cheesecake

Crust:
1/4 cup butter
2 cups crushed vanilla wafers
1/4 teaspoon ground cinnamon
1/4 teaspoon ground allspice

Filling:
1 lb. cream cheese, softened
1 cup sour cream
2/3 cup sugar
4 eggs, separated
2 tablespoons all-purpose flour
1/2 teaspoon vanilla extract
Finely grated peel and juice of 1 lemon

Garnish:
Powdered sugar

Preheat oven to 350F (175C). Grease a 9-inch springform pan. To prepare crust, melt butter in a small saucepan over low heat. Stir in crushed vanilla wafers and spices. press mixture in bottom of greased pan. Set aside. To prepare filling, beat cream cheese, sour cream, 1/3 cup of sugar, egg yolks, flour, vanilla nd lemon peel and juice in a large bowl until smooth. Beat egg whites with remaining sugar until soft peaks form; fold into cheese mixture. Spoon filling into prepared crust. Bake in preheated oven 1 hour or until set. Cool before removing from pan. To garnish, dust with powdered sugar.

Makes 10 to 12 servings.

Strawberry Cheesecake

Crust:
1/3 cup butter
1-3/4 cups crushed vanilla wafers

Filling:
8 oz. ricotta cheese
2/3 cup plain yogurt
2/3 cup sour cream
2 eggs, separated
Finely grated peel and juice of 1 orange
2 pint baskets strawberries, hulled
1 tablespoon plus 2 teaspoons unflavored gelatin
2 tablespoons water
1/4 cup sugar

Garnish:
2/3 cup whipping cream

Grease a 9-inch springform pan. To prepare crust, melt butter in a small saucepan over low heat. Stir in crushed vanilla wafers. Press mixture in bottom of greased pan. Set aside. To prepare filling, beat ricotta cheese, yogurt, sour cream, egg yolks and orange peel and juice in a large bowl until smooth. Reserve 10 strawberries. Process remaining strawberries in a food processor or blender 30 seconds or until pureed. Stir into cheese mixture. Combine gelatin with water in a small saucepan. Simmer until gelatin is completely dissolved; stir into cheese mixture. Beat egg whites with sugar until soft peaks form; fold into cheese mixture. Spoon filling into prepared crust. Refrigerate 2 to 3 hours or until set. To garnish, whip cream until stiff. Pipe (with a pastry bag) a border of 20 whipped cream rosettes around edge of cheesecake. Cut reserved strawberries in half. Top each rosette with a strawberry half.

Makes 8 to 10 servings.

Tutti Fruiti Cheesecake

12 oz. cream cheese, softened
1/4 cup sugar
2 eggs
1 tablespoon unflavored gelatin
2 tablespoons water
1/4 cup slivered almonds
2 tablespoons grated orange peel
2 tablespoons grated lemon peel
1/4 cup chopped raisins
3 tablespoons Grand Marnier or orange liqueur
1/4 cup chopped glacé cherries
28 to 30 ladyfinger cookies

Garnish:
5 glacé cherries, cut in half
Angelica pieces, cut in strips

Grease an 8" x 4" loaf pan. To prepare filling, beat cream cheese, sugar and eggs in a large bowl until smooth. Combine gelatin and water in a small saucepan. Simmer until gelatin is completely dissolved; stir into cheese mixture. Stir in almonds, orange and lemon peels, raisins. Grand Marnier or orange liqueur and cherries. Spoon filling into greased pan. Cut ladyfingers to fit into pan; arrange on filling. Refrigerate 2 to 3 hours or until set. Turn cheesecake out onto a serving dish. Garnish with cherry halves and angelica strips.

Makes 10 servings.

INDEX

P . 37
77